The Economics of Iterative Software Development

The Economics of Iterative Software Development

Steering Toward Better Business Results

Walker Royce
Kurt Bittner
Mike Perrow

✦✦Addison-Wesley

Upper Saddle River, NJ • Boston • Indianapolis • San Francisco
New York • Toronto • Montreal • London • Munich • Paris • Madrid
Capetown • Sydney • Tokyo • Singapore • Mexico City

The appendix is adapted from Spence/Bittner, *Managing Interative Software Development Projects*, © 2006 Pearson Education, Inc. Reproduced by permission of Pearson Education, Inc.

The publisher offers excellent discounts on this book when ordered in quantity for bulk purchases or special sales, which may include electronic versions and/or custom covers and content particular to your business, training goals, marketing focus, and branding interests. For more information, please contact U.S. Corporate and Government Sales, (800) 382-3419, corpsales@pearsontechgroup.com.

For sales outside the United States, please contact International Sales, international@pearson.com.

Visit us on the Web: informit.com/aw

Library of Congress Cataloging-in-Publication Data

Royce, Walker
  The economics of iterative software development : steering toward better business results / Walker Royce, Kurt Bittner, Mike Perrow.
    p.   cm.
  Includes bibliographical references and index.
  ISBN 978-0-321-50935-2 (hardcover : alk. paper)
  1. Computer software—Development—Management. 2. Software engineering. I. Bittner, Kurt. II. Perrow, Mike. III. Title.

  QA76.76.D47R685 2009
  005.1—dc22
                                                2009003221

ISBN-13: 978-0-321-50935-2
ISBN-10:   0-321-50935-8
Text printed in the United States on recycled paper at R.R. Donnelley in Crawfordsville, Indiana.
First printing, March 2009

For Barry Boehm, whose ideas have inspired us all.

CONTENTS

PREFACE

Imagine you're a wealthy, seasoned traveler planning a month-long, multi-country vacation. Sound nice? Go ahead, pick a continent, some part of the world you always wanted to explore. Where do you begin? If you had the luxury to actually consider such a notion, you might quickly determine your starting point and where you'd eventually end. You'd imagine a sequence of smaller journeys to famous cities, mountains, seaside resorts. But as you began scoping out the general profile of your trip, would you begin planning every meal, every evening stroll, every purchase you'd be making? Of course not. No one can plan in advance exactly what to do in all those unknown places, or exactly how to use the time and resources available along the way. Besides, you know that the quality of a journey is bound to suffer if you try sticking to rigid plans designed before you set out.

This book is about managing software development projects, which are seldom confused with long vacations. But from a management perspective, they have many things in common, all having to do with the unfamiliar—unfamiliar territory, languages, personal behavior, practices, costs, and infrastructure. This book is based on experiences that have involved thousands of miles of travel and thousands of hours of hard work alongside businesses whose software development teams encounter these uncertainties with every project. The most successful of these teams plan their projects at a high level first, then, like seasoned travelers, they plan in smaller steps called *iterations* as their journey progresses.

We attempt to explain those successes in terms most managers interested in improving business results will understand. With results in mind, we don't assume a great deal of technical experience on the part of the reader, but we do assume a commitment to successful leadership. This book targets readers who find themselves in leadership positions at various levels in a business organization, especially organizations that acquire, manage, or develop software as a component of business strategy. Our objective is to describe the benefits of frequent course correction during the iterative project, how to measure the interim results, and how the overall approach contributes meaningfully to the bottom line.

This last point has everything to do with the underlying theme of this book: economics. In the broadest sense, good economics means efficient management of finite resources toward an optimal result. Software economics is based on these same principles. We spend some time exploring poor economics based on old-fashioned management styles, including the inefficiencies that occur when software projects are managed as if they were traditional engineering projects, such as the construction of a bridge. When it comes to software construction, these inefficiencies are costly in terms of time, budget, and missed opportunities in the competitive marketplace. By contrast, modern iterative development methods will improve results based on practical governance of your team's finite resources; hence, the title of this book.

The order of our parts and chapters is straightforward. Part I, "The Software-Driven Economy," presents the context for software development and management in today's business climate, the difficulties of success, as well as the consequences of failure. Part II, "Improving Software Development Economics," focuses on a modern approach to software engineering based on the principles and practices of iterative development. We certainly don't know everything.

But through decades of observation we know what *doesn't* work, and we have learned quite a bit about what does. Part III, "Practical Measurement for Software Engineering," offers a more detailed look at how you can be sure these techniques work—through measurement. As an update on the tenet that "you can't manage what you can't measure," this final portion of the book focuses on the purposes of metrics, including the means by which variance can be reduced throughout the project lifecycle.

Whether you're a seasoned software project manager looking for a relatively brief review of iterative development principles, or a novice looking for a digestible introduction to these concepts, I think you'll find this book valuable.

Mike Perrow
Medford, Massachusetts

ABOUT THE AUTHORS

Walker Royce is the vice president of IBM's Worldwide Rational Services. He joined Rational in 1994 and served as vice president of Professional Services from 1997 through IBM's acquisition of Rational in 2003. He has managed large software engineering projects, consulted with a broad spectrum of IBM's worldwide customer base, and developed a software management approach that exploits an iterative life cycle, industry best practices, and architecture-first priorities. He is the author of *Software Project Management: A Unified Framework* (Addison-Wesley, 1998) and is a principal contributor to the management philosophy inherent in the Rational Unified Process. Before joining Rational, he spent 16 years in software project development, software technology development, and software management roles at TRW Electronics & Defense. He was a recipient of TRW's Chairman's Award for Innovation for his contributions in distributed architecture middleware and iterative software processes in 1990 and was named a TRW Technical Fellow in 1992. He received his BA in physics from the University of California, and his MS in computer information and control engineering from the University of Michigan.

Kurt Bittner is Chief Technical Officer for the Americas at Ivar Jacobson Consulting. He has worked in the software industry for more than 26 years in a variety of roles, including developer, team leader, architect, project manager, and business leader. He has led agile projects, run a large division of a software development company, survived and thrived in several start-ups, and worked with clients in a variety of industries including insurance, banking, and energy. He was a key contributor to the early development of the Rational Unified Process and, more recently, IBM's Jazz project (see www.jazz.net). His experience includes significant work in database-based system design and architecture, as well as consulting and mentoring a wide variety of clients on software development improvement strategies and approaches. He is the co-author of two books, *Use Case Modeling* (Addison-Wesley, 2003) and *Managing Iterative Software Development Projects* (Addison-Wesley, 2007), with Ian Spence, as well as many articles, especially in the areas of improving requirements and software development management practices.

Mike Perrow works as a writer and editor for the Rational organization within the IBM Software Group. He is the founding editor of *The Rational Edge* online magazine, which he helped create in 2000 when Rational was an independent company. In that role, he has worked closely with Rational methodologists and thought leaders, including Walker Royce, Kurt Bittner, and many others, to explain the concepts of iterative software development that underlie the Rational Unified Process and related toolset. He began his career as a technical writer on mainframe systems while teaching technical writing at Old Dominion University. Since then, he has taught periodically and served as an evangelist and marketer for Imagination Systems, Powersoft, and Sybase, Inc. In his parallel life as a creative writer, he has published poems in leading literary journals, including *The Southern Review, Shenandoah,* and *Boston Review.*

PART I
THE SOFTWARE-DRIVEN ECONOMY

Software is everywhere, and it is essential to the daily workings of the world in which we live. Everything we use seems to contain increasing amounts of software: from household appliances like microwave ovens and toasters, to consumer electronics, automobiles, and toys. All contain software that is essential to their operation.

Our health care system is heavily dependent on software to handle billing, patient record management, and in some cases patient care itself. To varying degrees, many of us rely on the accessibility of information over the Internet, as well as the capability to conduct online business.

Most businesses simply could not operate without the software systems that run their operations and enable their employees to collaborate.

1
. . .

THE CHALLENGE OF SOFTWARE PROJECT MANAGEMENT

Despite the increasing importance of software in our world, the average software project is maddeningly difficult to manage—schedules slip, projects fail, or if they're completed they frequently fail to deliver what was intended. These frustrations are well known to those of us whose jobs lie in the world of delivering software solutions; we all have our personal horror stories of projects gone awry. And given the importance of software today, such failures quickly translate into lost business opportunities, or even failed businesses.

Successful businesses, by contrast, understand the importance of software development capability as a means to ensure project health and long-term business viability. But companies that understand how to manage software development—whether to run their business systems for maximum advantage or to create software for the commercial market, or both—are rare. The truth is, most growing businesses are unprepared to create the software that defines how they interact with customers or helps deliver their goods and services.

Why? One reason is that most businesses still cling to an outdated model for their IT departments, treating them as an arms-length service provider that line-of-business managers must "contract" with for delivery of commodity services. Instead, software and the processes through which software is created should be considered a vital part of the business's value chain from the beginning. Software that is truly integrated into a company's business processes can change and improve the entire operation, as innovators such as Amazon.com and Apple have demonstrated. Given the growing benefits of integrating software capability into the business value chain, we need to change the traditional relationship corporate management has with IT.

At the level of executive leadership, software development capability must be understood as a core business competency if the benefits of game-changing innovation are to be realized. At the level of IT management, software projects must be understood as value propositions that strengthen the company's competitive posture, not simply feats of engineering.

In this first section, we will discuss the failures of IT to realize the potential of software innovation, some of the typical reasons for that failure, and introduce a new concept of *software management*— one that replaces traditional *software engineering* with a more practical approach grounded in software economics.

THE HIGH STAKES IN SOFTWARE DEVELOPMENT

We have come a long way since the 1980s when we believed that personal computing might have far-reaching implications for commerce, defense, and society in general. We have computing power that was unimagined even in the 1990s, that is, lightning-fast processing, ample memory, and virtually unlimited storage capacity. We also have extraordinary accessibility to the advantages this computing power can bring; we've managed to vastly simplify the user interface, making it ever easier to get email, access the Internet, or learn new software to improve our lives in various ways. Plus, we have previously unpredicted bandwidth, even if some consumers and segments of the Web are still not taking advantage of it yet. We are living in a world connected through both fixed lines and mobile devices to the rapidly growing Internet, which is enabling ever higher definition within a multitude of media, month by month.

Yet, despite the tremendous strides this industry has taken in computing power, we will not be able to take full advantage of those benefits until our software achieves similar levels of excellence. To say this another way, the world will not realize its digital potential until software systems rise to the level of capability exhibited in today's computing hardware and networks. The problem lies in the way software is developed.

INSTITUTIONAL FOCUS

We can measure some of the difficulties facing us in the area of software. The well-known CHAOS report from the Massachusetts-based Standish Group has measured the success/failure rate of software projects since their ground-breaking 1994 report, which indicated only 16.2% of all software projects succeeded in terms of budget projections, deadlines, and functionality. Although Standish's 2007 report indicates that the success rate has improved to 35%,[1] this still suggests that nearly two-thirds of all software projects are not completed as expected.

It's hard to imagine another field of engineering where such a poor success rate for funded, managed projects is considered normal, much less tolerated. To be sure, some in the industry[2] have questioned Standish's underlying assumptions about what constitutes "failure." How can a sector of the modern economy as vital as software be rife with project failure? The answer is complex, and

---

1. See David Rubenstein, "Standish Group Report: There's Less Development Chaos Today," SD Times, March 1, 2007 (at www.sdtimes.com).

2. See, for instance, www.infoq.com/news/Standish-Chaos-Report-Questioned.

goes to the heart of what we mean by the term *engineering*. We will discuss this term in the following pages. For now, the salient fact is the amount of attention Standish's annual study receives, because it underscores the frustrations of software project managers seeking ways to improve their project results, which, they admit, are much worse than they had hoped for.

Although the Standish Group points out failures, other professional organizations such as the Project Management Institute (PMI), the Institute of Electrical and Electronics Engineers, Inc. (IEEE), the Software Engineering Institute (SEI), and the IBM Rational organization devote a significant share of their resources specifically to improving the management of software projects. The PMI's Project Management Body of Knowledge, or PMBOK, is a well-known guide in navigating the complexities inherent in software projects. The IEEE, long considered the world's leading professional authority regarding all forms of engineering technology, publishes some of the software industry's most respected publications focused on best practices in software project management. The SEI's Capability Maturity Management Integration (CMMI) guideline has evolved as the gold standard for measuring organizational capability regarding software development, especially in the defense industry. And under its Rational software brand, IBM promotes the Rational Unified Process as a framework of practices that can be tailored to all sizes of software development organizational needs.

In addition to these organizations, software professionals frequently consult guidelines published under banners such as Six Sigma, originated at Motorola as a set of practices geared toward defect reduction, and Lean Manufacturing, a concept pioneered by Toyota for the elimination of waste in the manufacturing process. Neither Lean nor Six Sigma were designed specifically for the software industry, but a persistent interest in resolving the difficulties of software project management regularly motivates industry leaders and practitioners to consider a variety of guidelines developed for project management in general.

Also, since 2000, the difficulties inherent in software projects have produced a variety of new approaches by various organizations and professional federations, such as the Agile Alliance, the Scrum Alliance, the eXtreme Programming community, not to mention various open-source (noncommercial) projects such as OpenUP (the Open Unified Process). Each of these organizations promotes different development methods, each with merits for particular software development teams whose size, style, and collective degree of experience may suggest one method as more appropriate than another.

Despite the different perspectives and goals of these professional organizations and companies, their methods underline a common purpose: to overcome the inadequacies of traditional software development techniques prevalent since the 1960s. The overriding distinction between these new approaches and the more traditional approach can be summed up as follows: The new ways represent *iterative and incremental* development practice, whereas the old ways represent *waterfall* development practice. To some, this may seem a gross characterization, but the distinction is fair enough and will serve our purposes here.

Next, we take a look at traditional waterfall development, and then describe the ways in which modern, iterative development practices offer improvements.

TRADITIONAL SOFTWARE PROJECT MANAGEMENT

In the old way of thinking about software project management, a project is broken into distinct phases. You develop a detailed plan of activities, track that plan's execution, and adjust for variances between planned performance and actual performance. Traditionally, you assess a plan's quality by scrutinizing its level of detail. There's little uncertainty about the steps or the eventual outcome in the construction industry, for example, where the laws of physics, properties of materials, and maturity of building codes and practices are established engineering disciplines. Success simply depends on resource management.

But in the software-development industry, these traditional methods cause a huge percentage of software-development projects to founder. True, a sequential, activity-based construction approach may be better than nothing, but the success rate for software projects following this approach — typically called the waterfall model — is about 1 in 10.

As we've already noted, the reasons for this failure are not readily apparent to those schooled in the practices of traditional engineering. Indeed, it's tempting to compare software construction to the building of a house. Both projects involve requirements management, design (blueprints), scheduling, specialty teams (comparable to roofers, carpenters, plumbers, etc.), and inspections.

But decades of software projects have shown us that traditional modes of construction are very different from the diverse ways in which software is designed and delivered to the customer. One reason for software's low success rate (refer to the Standish report) is that traditional project-management approaches do not account for the level of creativity often required to complete software projects that are initiated with significant levels of uncertainty regarding project essentials, including

- The problem. What the user really wants or needs
- The solution. What architecture and technology mix is most appropriate
- The planning. Cost and time constraints, team composition, stakeholder communication, desirable phases, etc.

PROBLEMS WITH THE WATERFALL APPROACH

The traditional waterfall approach to project management is a sequential, activity-based paradigm. In this approach, activities cascade from requirements gathering, to design, followed by coding activities, then unit testing, integration activities, and finally system acceptance. Here are 10 classic rules that waterfall adherents cling to:

1. Freeze requirements before design.
2. Avoid coding before detailed design review.
3. Use a higher-order programming language.
4. Complete unit testing before integration.
5. Maintain detailed traceability among all artifacts.
6. Document and maintain the design.
7. Assess quality with an independent team.
8. Inspect everything.
9. Plan everything early with high precision.
10. Control source code baselines rigorously.

As noted earlier, these principles align with traditional construction methods. Don't do any blueprints until you've got every detail discussed and approved with the owner; don't build anything until the owner has totally approved the blueprints; pneumatic nail guns are better than hammers for the bulk of construction; buy standard plumbing fixtures, toilets, appliance, and electrical fixtures and they will install and integrate with no issues; require city building inspectors at each major milestone to ensure compatibility with established codes. And yes, this is a fine way to go about business — *unless you're building software*.

Consider the practical limitations of the 10 classic rules listed above. Gathering software requirements before starting the design process makes sense; but finalizing and freezing these requirements as a first milestone, as if everything about a system's function and feature set can be known up front, has proved to be a major pitfall for countless projects.

For example: In a typical scenario for a small- to medium-size waterfall-driven software project, a group of stakeholders and one or more software analysts begin with a high-level set of requirements.

Over time—say, six weeks—they refine the requirements to some level of granularity based on their best understanding of their users' needs and their business objectives. But soon, prudence dictates that the actual design process must begin; management assumes that all requirements are sufficiently well known and that it's time to stop that process and move to the design stage.

The next team moves in to elaborate the design according to the completed set of requirements, and after a few months they turn their design over to the construction team who writes code according to the design. After many months, the coding team delivers all or major portions to the test team. Testers find bugs in the code, which is to be expected. What the project manager doesn't expect is the reaction from stakeholders, who, more than a year after the project began, are now seeing the first versions of the software, which does not resemble what they thought their requirements specified, and moreover does not meet their current needs.

What went wrong? How could adhering to a plan produce such a poor product?

First, the problem begins in the nature of the planning. In gathering requirements, it's simply not useful to hone them to five digits of precision when the stakeholders have only a one-digit-of-precision understanding of the problem, solution, or plan. A prolonged requirements-gathering effort at the beginning of a project may be well intentioned; but taking time to build precise requirements as the first step only delays a more thorough understanding of the real problems that lie ahead in building the system—problems that we call "the architecturally significant issues."

Second, solutions evolve from *user specifications*, and user specifications evolve from *candidate solutions* (which is why there's no point in trying to get all the requirements right early on). Candidate solutions—demonstrations of working software portions that will evolve into a more elaborate system—need to be presented frequently to stakeholders. Those who are footing the bill, or have a final say in the project, usually maintain their right to revise requirements specified earlier. Most stakeholders don't really know what they want until they begin to see something functional, so teams should demonstrate their incremental results early and often. This is at the heart of what we mean by "iterative" software development.

Third, software projects typically fail when project managers focus on the *activities* of their specialized teams and team members instead of their *results*. We'll discuss this in more depth in the second section of this book. In the context of iterative development, a results focus leads to smaller teams working on smaller chunks of code over short durations. In the typical waterfall project outlined earlier, a very large team works on the entire system over a period of a year or more. Yet in the end, all the activities involved in requirements, design, coding, and testing yielded a single, failed result.

These are only three of the most obvious problems that plague most waterfall-based projects, and as you can see, they are all closely related. The very metaphor of a waterfall holds a major key to the problem—a stream flows downhill from surface to surface, and gravity will not allow progress to stop temporarily in order to revisit upstream activities.

SUMMARY

Software processes should be considered a vital part of a business's value chain, extending from the IT department, through business operations, and into the marketplace where successful businesses differentiate themselves from their competition. Innovators such as Amazon.com and Apple have demonstrated the power of software integrated fully into the business model. Most modern corporations could adopt this strategy, but the traditional relationship corporate management has with IT—whereby software projects are controlled by rigid processes and measured according to predetermined requirements—limits the possibilities.

A new approach to software development and delivery should consider that

- Software development is itself an innovative process. Confronting problems and risks through planning is a necessary first step, but managing the project according to early and overly precise assumptions is a waste of time. A more thorough understanding of the real problems lies ahead in building the system, when "the architecturally significant issues" are discovered and addressed.
- Most stakeholders don't know what they want from a software system until they see it in action. An iterative approach to building a new system allows stakeholders to change their minds about early requirements, and allows software development teams the chance to demonstrate creative solutions to evolving needs.
- Achieving results is more important than performing activities as part of a process. Results can be achieved in stages, and they can be demonstrated via working software long before the final system is complete.

We've spent the first chapter describing some of the basic problems in software development. Now let's take a closer look at an alternative approach to software project management.

2
. . .
ACHIEVING RESULTS: THE CASE FOR SOFTWARE ECONOMICS

Uncertainty is inherent in the nature of software projects. That is far less likely to be the case in building a bridge over a river, at least in terms of what the structure is designed to accomplish. Philippe Kruchten points to the "soft" in "software,"[1] noting that software requirements (what a system is required to do) usually change over the course of completion. This is why we've said it's counterproductive to require high precision in the design when the development team has low precision in their understanding of the problem.

We need a modern way of thinking about software-quality management that accommodates our industry's 30 years of lessons learned and patterns of successful projects. Today's most successful software-management techniques steer software projects through the minefield of "uncertainties" rather than tracking against a precise long-term plan. Delivering innovation on schedule and on budget requires iterative lifecycles, constant risk management, objective

---

1. See Philippe Kruchten's article, "The nature of software: What's so special about software engineering?" www.ibm.com/developerworks/rational/library/4700.html, where he discusses "the soft, but rather unkind, nature of software."

oversight, and a "steering" style of leadership that demands creativity throughout the team, however large or small.

If you consider a Hollywood movie production, this mode of project management may make more immediate sense. Movie producers regularly create a unique and complex web of intellectual property bounded only by a vision and human creativity. We can easily imagine that the economic performance of movie production looks pretty similar to the economic performance of software projects: Since 2000, about one in three delivers on budget and on schedule with any sort of predictability.[2]

Like the movie industry, we need qualified architects (directors), analysts (scriptwriters, designers), software engineers (production crews, editors, special effects producers, actors, stunt doubles), and project managers (producers). Also like the movie industry, we must get increments of software into executable form (get it on film) to make things tangible enough to assess progress and quality. There is a lot of scrap and rework in this process as we discover what works and what does not, and we synthesize the contributions of many people into one cohesive piece of integrated intellectual property.

No doubt these observations sound countercultural to project managers who use traditional engineering practices to produce airplanes, bridges, heart transplant valves, nuclear reactors, skyscrapers, and satellites. But what we have learned is that software management is more accurately described as a discipline of software *economics* rather than software *engineering*. Day-to-day decisions by software managers (like those of movie producers) are dominated by value judgments, cost tradeoffs, human factors, macro-economic trends, technology trends, market strength, and timing. Software projects are rarely concerned with precise mathematics, material properties, laws of physics, or established and mature engineering tenets.

---

2. Standish Group International, Inc., *Chaos Chronicles*, 2004.

ITERATIVE DEVELOPMENT

Modern software management methods—generally known as *iterative* development methods—have begun to take these differences into consideration. Rather than tracking against a precise, long-term plan, the iterative method steers software projects through the minefield of uncertainties inherent in developing today's software applications, products, and services. Successfully delivering software products on schedule and on budget requires an evolving mixture of discovery, production, assessment, and a *steering* leadership style. The word *steering* implies active management involvement and frequent course-correction to produce better results. All stakeholders must collaborate to converge on moving targets.

The IBM Rational Unified Process,[3] a well-accepted benchmark of a modern iterative development process, provides a framework for a more balanced evolution that encourages the management of uncertainty and risk. Its lifecycle includes four phases, each with a demonstrable result:

1. **Inception:** Definition and prototype of the vision and business case
2. **Elaboration:** Synthesis, demonstration, and assessment of an architecture baseline
3. **Construction:** Development, demonstration, and assessment of useful increments
4. **Transition:** Usability assessment, final production, and deployment

The phase names represent the state of the project rather than a sequential-activity-based progression from requirements to design to code to test to delivery.

We call this iterative management style *results*-based rather than *activity*-based. In the world of software, real results are executable

---

3. See, for example, Per Kroll and Philippe Krutchten, *The Rational Unified Process Made Easy: A Practitioner's Guide*. Addison-Wesley Longman, 2003.

programs. Everything else (requirements documents, use case models, design models, test cases, plans, processes, documentation, inspections) is secondary, and simply part of the means to the end: an executable software program.

For those of you with coding experience, think back to your programmer days: When you were building a model, sketching a flowchart, reasoning through logic of a state machine, or composing source code, you knew you were simply speculating and synthesizing an abstract solution. It wasn't very tangible until you got it to compile, link, and execute; then you could truly reason about its quality, performance, usefulness, and completeness. Project managers should feel the same way. As long as you are assessing the beauty or goodness of a plan, model, document, or some other nonexecutable representation, you are only *speculating* about quality and progress. Movie producers feel the same way about scripts, storyboards, set mockups, and costume designs. They commit scenes to film to make the presentation tangible enough that they can judge its overall integrated effect.

BENEFITS OF THE RESULTS-BASED APPROACH

Iterative development techniques, industry best practices, and economic motivations drive software-development companies to take a more results-based approach. Develop the business case and vision and prototype the solution; elaborate this into a basic architecture; create usable, iterative releases; and then finalize into field-ready code. Here are the top 10 principles of results-based software development:

- **Use an architecture-first approach.** An early focus on the architecture results in a solid foundation for 20% of the stuff (requirements, components, user interactions, project risks, etc.) that drives the overall success of the project. Get the architecturally important things to be well understood and stable before worrying about the complete breadth and depth of all the artifacts, and you'll see far less scrap and rework over the course of the project.

- **Confront risks early.** Resolving the critical issues first results in a predictable production with fewer surprises to impact your budget and schedule.
- **Establish a change-management environment.** Along with the advantages of iterative development comes the need to carefully manage changes to artifacts over the course of the project.
- **Enhance change freedom through collaborative environments.** Without substantial automation of the bookkeeping, change management, documentation, traceability, metrics collection, testing, and status reporting, it is difficult to reduce iteration cycles to manageable time frames so that change is encouraged rather than avoided.
- **Design software with rigorous, model-based notation.** An engineering notation for design enables complexity control, objective assessment, and automated analyses.
- **Instrument the process for objective quality control.** Progress and quality indicators are derived directly from the evolving artifacts for more meaningful insight into trends and correlation with requirements.
- **Employ demonstration-based approaches for intermediate assessment of progress and quality.** Executable demonstrations of relevant scenarios stimulate earlier convergence on integration and understanding of the tradeoffs between requirements, design, and planning constraints.
- **Plan releases with evolving levels of detail.** Each project increment and demonstration should reflect current levels of detail for both requirements and architecture, since these things evolve in balance. What's more, the level of precision

in the software evolves along with the level of understanding of the project team.

- **Establish a scalable, configurable process.** No single process is suitable for all software-development projects. To be pragmatic, a process framework needs to be configurable for a broad spectrum of applications. This ensures economy of scale and best return on investment.

THE MARK OF SUCCESS

The most discriminating characteristic of a successful software-development process is a well-defined separation between "research-and-development" activities and "production" activities. When software projects do not succeed, the primary reason is usually a failure to crisply define and execute these two stages, with proper balance and appropriate emphasis. This is true for both traditional (waterfall) and iterative processes. Most unsuccessful projects exhibit one of these characteristics:

- An overemphasis on the R&D aspects. Teams perform too many analyses or paper studies, or procrastinate on the construction of engineering baselines.
- An overemphasis on the production aspects through rush-to-judgment designs, premature work by overeager coders, and continuous hacking.

By contrast, successful projects tend to have very well-defined project milestones in which there's a noticeable transition from a research attitude to a production attitude. Earlier phases focus on achieving functionality; later phases revolve around achieving a product that can be shipped to a customer.

Software management is hard work. Technical breakthroughs, process breakthroughs, and new tools will make it easier, but management discipline will continue to be the crux of software-project success. New technological advances will be accompanied by new opportunities for software applications, new complexities, new modes of automation, and new customers with different priorities.

Accommodating these changes will perturb many of our ingrained software-management values and priorities. However, striking a balance among requirements, designs, and plans will remain the underlying objective of future software-management endeavors, just as it is today.

SUMMARY

Think of a software project as you might think of a movie production. You begin with a general sense of purpose, a budget, a crew, but you don't really know how successful your efforts are until you review the reels at the end of the day. Iterative software development takes a similar approach to results, one increment at a time. You not only demonstrate progress to stakeholders, but you can address the really hard things first in order to show the project's value and feasibility sooner rather than later.

This is the essence of results-based software development. It allows you to steer a project toward a more successful conclusion, because you assess where you are in terms of tangible, demonstratable results more frequently than with traditional techniques based on extensive up-front design.

Parts II and III of this book will explore the results-based approach to managing software development projects in the context of software economics. Part II presents the general concepts and techniques that successful project teams embrace as they become skilled in iterative, incremental development. Part III describes how you can be assured that these techniques are working, through steady and systematic measurement during the development process.

PART II
IMPROVING SOFTWARE
DEVELOPMENT ECONOMICS

For more than 20 years, we have been working with the world's largest software development organizations across the entire spectrum of software domains, harvesting and synthesizing lessons from in-the-trenches experience. We have diagnosed the symptoms of many successful and unsuccessful projects, and we have identified root causes of recurring problems and their solutions.

One of our primary goals has been to apply what we've learned in order to enable software development organizations to make substantial improvements in their software project economics and organizational capabilities. In Part II of this book, we will summarize the key approaches that deliver these benefits.

3

. . .

TRENDS IN SOFTWARE ECONOMICS

Over the past two decades, the software industry has moved progressively toward new methods for managing the ever-increasing complexity of software projects. We have seen evolutions and revolutions, with varying degrees of success and failure. Although software technologies, processes, and methods have advanced rapidly, software engineering remains a people-intensive process. Consequently, techniques for managing people, technology, resources, and risks have profound leverage.

The early software approaches of the 1960s and 1970s can best be described as craftsmanship, with each project using custom or ad-hoc processes and custom tools that were quite simple in their scope. By the 1980s and 1990s, the software industry had matured and was starting to exhibit signs of becoming more of an engineering discipline. However, most software projects in this era were still primarily exploring new technologies and approaches that were largely unpredictable in their results and marked by diseconomies of scale. In recent years, however, new techniques that aggressively attack project risk, leverage automation to a greater degree, and exhibit much-improved economies of scale have begun to grow in acceptance. Much-improved software economics are already being achieved by leading software organizations who use these approaches.

Let's take a look at one successful model for describing software economics.

A SIMPLIFIED MODEL OF SOFTWARE ECONOMICS

There are several software cost models in use today. The most popular, open, and well-documented model is the COnstructive COst MOdel (COCOMO), which has been widely used by the industry for 20 years. The latest version, COCOMO II, is the result of a collaborative effort led by the University of Southern California (USC) Center for Software Engineering, with the financial and technical support of numerous industry affiliates. The objectives of this team are threefold:

- To develop a software cost and schedule estimation model for the lifecycle practices of the post-2000 era
- To develop a software project database and tool support for improvement of the cost model
- To provide a quantitative analytic framework for evaluating software technologies and their economic impacts

The accuracy of COCOMO II allows its users to estimate cost within 30% of actuals, 74% of the time. This level of unpredictability in the outcome of a software development process should be truly frightening to any software project investor, especially in view of the fact that few projects ever perform better than expected.

The COCOMO II cost model includes numerous parameters and techniques for estimating a wide variety of software development projects. For the purposes of this discussion, we will abstract COCOMO II into a function of four basic parameters:

- **Complexity.** The complexity of the software solution is typically quantified in terms of the size of human-generated components (the number of source instructions or the number of function points) needed to develop the features in a usable product.
- **Process.** This refers to the process used to produce the end product, and in particular its effectiveness in helping developers avoid "overhead" activities.
- **Team.** This refers to the capabilities of the software engineering team, and particularly their experience with both the computer science issues and the application domain issues for the project at hand.
- **Tools.** This refers to the software tools a team uses for development—that is, the extent of process automation.

The relationships among these parameters in modeling the estimated effort can be expressed as follows:

$$\text{Effort} = (\text{Team}) \times (\text{Tools}) \times (\text{Complexity})^{(\text{Process})}$$

Schedule estimates are computed directly from the effort estimate and process parameters. Reductions in effort generally result in reductions in schedule estimates. To simplify this discussion, we can assume that the "cost" includes both effort and time. The complete COCOMO II model includes several modes, numerous parameters, and several equations. This simplified model enables us to focus the discussion on the more discriminating dimensions of improvement.

What constitutes a good software cost estimate is a very tough question. In our experience, a good estimate can be defined as one that has the following attributes:

- It is conceived and supported by a team accountable for performing the work, consisting of the project manager, the architecture team, the development team, and the test team.

- It is accepted by all stakeholders as ambitious but realizable.
- It is based on a well-defined software cost model with a credible basis and a database of relevant project experience that includes similar processes, similar technologies, similar environments, similar quality requirements, and similar people.
- It is defined in enough detail for both developers and managers to objectively assess the probability of success and to understand key risk areas.

Although several parametric models have been developed to estimate software costs, they can all be generally abstracted into the form given above. One very important aspect of software economics (as represented within today's software cost models) is that the relationship between effort and size exhibits a diseconomy of scale. The software development diseconomy of scale is a result of the "process" exponent in the equation being greater than 1.0. In contrast to the economics for most manufacturing processes, the more software you build, the greater the cost per unit item. It is desirable, therefore, to reduce the size and complexity of a project whenever possible.

SOFTWARE ENGINEERING: A 40-YEAR HISTORY

Software engineering is dominated by intellectual activities focused on solving problems with immense complexity and numerous unknowns in competing perspectives. We can characterize three generations of software development as follows:

1. *1960s and 1970s: Craftsmanship.* Organizations used virtually all custom tools, custom processes, and custom components built in primitive languages. Project performance

was highly predictable but poor: Cost, schedule, and quality objectives were almost never met.

2. *1980s and 1990s: Early Software Engineering.* Organizations used more repeatable processes, off-the-shelf tools, and about 70% of their components were built in higher level languages. About 30% of these components were available as commercial products, including the operating system, database management system, networking, and graphical user interface. During the 1980s, some organizations began achieving economies of scale, but with the growth in applications' complexity (primarily in the move to distributed systems), the existing languages, techniques, and technologies were simply insufficient.

3. *2000 and later: Modern Software Engineering.* Modern practice is rooted in the use of managed and measured processes, integrated automation environments, and mostly (70%) off-the-shelf components. Typically, only about 30% of components need to be custom built.

Figure 3.1 illustrates the economics associated with these three generations of software development. The ordinate of the graph refers to software unit costs (per source line of code [SLOC], per function point, per component—take your pick) realized by an organization. The abscissa represents the lifecycle growth in the complexity of software applications developed by the organization.

Technologies for achieving reductions in complexity/size, process improvements, improvements in team effectiveness, and tool automation are not independent of one another. In each new generation, the key is complementary growth in all technologies. For example, in modern approaches, process advances cannot not be used successfully without component technologies and tool automation.

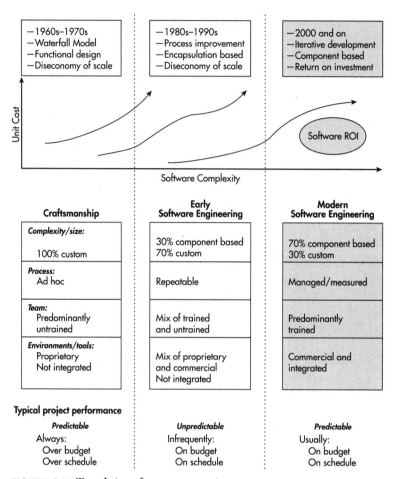

FIGURE 3.1 Trends in software economics

KEYS TO IMPROVEMENT: A BALANCED APPROACH

Improvements in the economics of software development have been not only difficult to achieve, but also difficult to measure and substantiate. In software textbooks, trade journals, and market literature, the topic of software economics is plagued by inconsistent jargon, inconsistent units of measure, disagreement among experts, and unending hyperbole. If we examine only one aspect of improving software economics, we are able to draw only narrow conclusions. Likewise, if an organization focuses on improving only one aspect of its software development process, it will not realize any significant economic improvement—even though it may make spectacular improvements in this single aspect of the process.

The key to substantial improvement in business performance is a balanced attack across the four basic parameters of the simplified software cost model: complexity, process, team, and tools. These parameters are in priority order for most software domains. In our experience, the following discriminating approaches have made a difference in improving the economics of software development and integration:

1. Reduce the size or complexity of what needs to be developed.
   - Reduce the amount of developed code by understanding business needs and delivering only that which is absolutely essential to satisfying those needs.
   - Reduce the amount of human-generated code through component-based technology and use of higher levels of abstraction.
   - Reuse existing functionality, whether through direct code reuse or use of service-oriented architectures.
   - Reduce the amount of functionality delivered in a single release to shorten the release cycle and reduce complexity; deliver increments of functionality in a series of releases.

2. Improve the development process.
   - Reduce scrap and rework by transitioning from a waterfall process to a modern, iterative development process.
   - Attack significant risks early through an architecture-first focus.
   - Evaluate areas of inefficiency and ineffectiveness and improve practices in response.

3. Create more proficient teams.
   - Improve individual skills.
   - Improve team interactions.
   - Improve organizational capability.

4. Use integrated tools that exploit more automation.
   - Improve human productivity through advanced levels of automation.
   - Eliminate sources of human error.
   - Support improvements in areas of process weakness.

Most software experts would also stress the significant dependencies among these trends. For example, new tools enable complexity reduction and process improvements; size-reduction approaches lead to process changes; and process improvements drive tool advances.

In addition, IT executives need to consider other trends in software economics whose importance is increasing. These include the lifecycle effects of commercial components-based solutions and rapid development (often a source of maintenance headaches); the effects of service-oriented architectures; the effects of user priorities and value propositions (often keys to business case analysis and to the management of scope and expectations); and the effects of stakeholder/team collaboration and shared vision achievement (often keys to rapid adaptation to changes in the IT marketplace).

SUMMARY

The evolution of software project management since the 1960s has moved through the stages of individual craftsmanship, through the application of engineering principles, to the beginnings of repeatable, somewhat predictable processes based on a better understanding of project risk coupled with the use of automation in the process.

This rise in predictability has allowed the emergence of cost estimation techniques, the most popular of which is COCOMO II.

The cost of a software project can best be estimated in terms of the four essential COCOMO II parameters: complexity, process, teams, and tools. Cost improvements result when the following occur:

1. Complexity can be reduced, either in the finished product or in the iterations produced during the project lifecycle.
2. The process can be improved by addressing risks first and reducing human error through automation.
3. Teams can become more efficient through skill enhancement and improved communication.
4. Automated tools can be used to heighten productivity and strengthen areas of the process.

In the next sections, we will elaborate on the approaches listed above for achieving improvements in each of the four dimensions. These approaches represent patterns of success we have observed among successful software development organizations that have made dramatic leaps in improving the economics of their software development efforts.

4

• • •

REDUCING SOFTWARE PROJECT SIZE
OR COMPLEXITY

The most significant way to improve economic results is usually to achieve a software solution with the minimum amount of human-generated source material. Our experience shows that managing scope and raising the level of abstraction through component-based technology and service-oriented architectures are the highest leverage techniques that make a difference.

MANAGING SCOPE

The scope of a software product is usually defined by a set of features, use cases, or requirements that specify what the product needs to do and how well it needs to do it. Managing scope requires an understanding of the real needs of the business and whether the "requirements" actually deliver the value required by the business, as well as the economic tradeoffs inherent in a set of features or requirements. It is essential to understand the relative value and cost of achieving each unit of scope. Typically, the development cost and economic value associated with the required product features are poorly understood in the early phases of a project, but they evolve and become clearer with time.

Consider a trivial product with four features, as represented in Figure 4.1. This illustration abstracts the units of cost, value, and economic leverage to simplify a very complex and context-dependent discipline. In most applications, representations of cost, value, and economic leverage assessments do not need to be precise to manage scope. They could be as simple as "low, moderate, high," or they could be represented by an integer ranging from 1 to 10, as in the illustration. The main point is that all requirements are not created equal. To manage scope, the units of scope need to be objectively differentiated. Simple coarse-grained assessments are usually good enough to make most of the significant decisions. Obvious conclusions to be drawn from the Figure 4.1 tradeoffs are that delivering a subset of the features faster may be a highly desirable option for the end product, or that a certain subset of features constitutes the best target for the first increment of capability demonstration.

Most products are not so trivial. A product might consist of tens, hundreds, or even thousands of requirements that are often interrelated and cannot simply be added to or subtracted from the scope; scenarios are typically better units of scoping as they provide something that can be executed end-to-end. Nevertheless, if you recognize the relative importance of different requirements and define some simple objective measures of cost and value for each

Required Feature	Cost	Value
A	1	2
B	3	7
C	4	5
D	5	4

Product Option 1: Produce All Features A, B, C, and D
Development Cost = 13, User Value = 18
Development Time = 14 months
Economic Leverage: 18/13 = 1.4

Product Option 2: Produce Only Features B and C
Development Cost = 7, User Value = 12
Development Time = 8 Months
Economic Leverage: 12/7 = 1.7

FIGURE 4.1 Tradeoffs in managing scope

unit of scope, you will succeed in managing scope and evolving a product toward a solution with more optimal economic leverage.

REDUCING THE SIZE OF HUMAN-GENERATED CODE

Component-based technology is a general term for reducing the size and complexity of human-generated code necessary to achieve a software solution. Commercial components, domain-specific reuse, architectural patterns, and higher-order programming languages are all elements of component-based approaches focused on achieving a given system with fewer lines of human-specified source directives (statements). For example, to achieve a certain application with a fixed number of features, we could use any of the following potential solutions:

- Develop 1,000,000 lines of custom assembly language.
- Develop 400,000 lines of custom C++.
- Develop 100,000 lines of custom C++, integrate 200,000 lines of existing reusable components, and purchase a commercial middleware product.
- Develop 50,000 lines of custom C# and purchase and integrate several commercial components on a .Net platform.
- Develop 5,000 lines of custom Java, develop 10,000 lines of custom HTML, and purchase and integrate several commercial components on a J2EE platform.

Sequentially, each of these solutions represents a step up in exploiting component-based technology and a commensurate reduction in the total amount of human-developed code, which in turn reduces the time and the team size needed for development. Since the difference between large and small projects has a greater-than-linear impact on the lifecycle cost, the use of the highest-level language and appropriate commercial components has the highest potential cost impact. Furthermore, simpler is generally better.

Reducing the size of custom-developed software usually increases understandability, reliability, and the ease of making changes.

IMPROVING REUSE USING SERVICE-ORIENTED ARCHITECTURES

Very few software projects exist in a vacuum; most need to interoperate with existing applications to one degree or another. Historically, this has been done using application programming interfaces, or APIs, that require alignments of programming models and technologies at a granular level of technology. As a result, application integration has been difficult and resource-intensive as well as a great source of errors. Service-oriented architectures (SOA) wrap this complexity with technology that allows applications, including those developed using different technologies, to be viewed as providers and consumers of services. This simplification reduces the complexity of the programming model and provides a way of viewing applications as large-grained components, thereby achieving many of the same benefits of component-based technology but on top of existing applications. SOA also enables existing applications to be evolved in a less disruptive way, reducing the overall cost of maintaining and enhancing applications. With up to 70% of most IT budgets consumed by maintaining and enhancing existing applications, SOA can have a significant effect on software economics.

SUMMARY

Reducing software project complexity, or size, is best achieved by minimizing the amount of human-generated material. This means reducing the number of lines of code created by reducing the project to its essential functionality. There are three prescriptions here: manage project scope, reduce handwritten computer code, and adopt strategies for code reuse so that previous solutions can serve as the basis for more advanced problems later.

Managing project scope effectively requires an understanding of the real needs of the business, not simply the requirements specified early on. Meeting some requirements may not yield value in proportion to the effort, whereas other requirements are quite valuable. Recognizing the relative value of each requirement will help determine the optimum project scope and the proper allocation of development resources.

Reducing the number of lines of custom-developed software code will also reduce project complexity. The more preexisting components can be leveraged for the project, the fewer lines of new and potentially error-prone code will be required. Similarly, proper use of a service-oriented architecture will simplify the use of existing technology by providing access to functionality without interrupting business processes or adding to maintenance costs.

Reducing complexity is a critical ingredient in improving software project health, and it paves the way toward the next goal, improving the development process.

5
. . .
IMPROVING THE DEVELOPMENT
PROCESS

In order to achieve success, real-world software projects require an incredibly complex web of both sequential and parallel steps. As the scale of the project increases, more overhead steps must be included just to manage the complexity of this web.

PROJECT PROCESSES

All project processes consist of productive activities and overhead activities.

Productive activities result in tangible progress toward the end product. For software efforts, these activities include prototyping, modeling, coding, integration, debugging, and user documentation.

Overhead activities have an intangible impact on the end product. They include plan preparation, requirements elicitation and management, documentation, progress monitoring, risk assessment, financial assessment, configuration control, quality assessment, testing, late scrap and rework, management, personnel training, business administration, and other tasks. Although overhead activities include many value-added efforts, in general, when less effort is devoted to these activities, more effort can be expended on productive activities.

The main thrust of process improvement is to improve the results of productive activities and minimize the impact of overhead activities on personnel and schedule. Based on our observations, these are the three most discriminating approaches for achieving significant process improvements:

- Transitioning to an iterative process.
- Attacking the significant risks first through a component-based, architecture-first focus.
- Improving software engineering practices used by teams, and looking for performance gaps. Typical practices needed by all teams include requirements elicitation and management, visual modeling, change management, and assessing quality throughout the lifecycle.

USING AN ITERATIVE PROCESS

The key discriminator in significant process improvement is making the transition from the conventional (waterfall) approach to a modern, iterative approach. The traditional software process was characterized by transitioning through sequential phases, from requirements to design to code to test, achieving 100% completion of each artifact at each lifecycle stage. All requirements, artifacts, components, and activities were treated as equally important. The goal was to achieve high-fidelity traceability among all artifacts at each stage in the lifecycle.

In practice, the traditional process resulted in

- Late agreement on the requirements
- Protracted integration and late design breakage
- Late risk resolution

- Requirements-driven functional decomposition
- Adversarial stakeholder relationships
- Focus on documents and review meetings

These symptoms almost always led to a significant diseconomy of scale, especially for larger projects involving many developers. By contrast, a modern (iterative) development process framework is characterized by

1. Continuous round-trip engineering from requirements to test, at evolving levels of abstraction
2. Achieving high-fidelity understanding of the architecturally significant decisions as early as practical
3. Evolving the artifacts in breadth and depth based on risk management priorities
4. Postponing completeness and consistency analyses until later in the lifecycle

A modern process framework attacks the primary sources of the diseconomy of scale inherent in the conventional software process.

Figure 5.1 provides an objective perspective of the difference between the conventional waterfall process and a modern iterative process. It graphs development progress versus time, where progress is defined as percent coded—that is, demonstrable in its target form. At that point, the software is compilable and executable. It is not necessarily complete, compliant, nor up to specifications.

In the waterfall project lifecycle, software development typically progressed without delivering any executable result until the integration phase. Requirements were first captured in complete detail in ad hoc text. Design documents were then fully elaborated in ad hoc notations. Coding and unit testing of individual components followed. Finally, the components were compiled and linked together into a complete system. This integration activity was the first time that significant inconsistencies among components (their

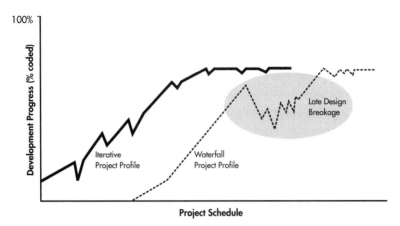

FIGURE 5.1 Project profiles for the waterfall and iterative processes

interfaces and behavior) could be tangibly recognized. These inconsistencies, some of which were extremely difficult to uncover, resulted from using ambiguous formats for the early lifecycle artifacts. Getting the software to operate reliably enough to test its usefulness took much longer than planned. Budget and schedule pressure drove teams to shoehorn in the quickest fixes; redesign was usually out of the question. Then the testing of system threads, usefulness, requirements compliance, and quality was performed through a series of releases until the software was judged adequate for the user. About 90% of the time, the end result was a software system that was late, over budget, fragile, and expensive to maintain.

A review of numerous conventional projects that followed a waterfall model shows a recurring symptom: Although it was not usually planned this way, the resources expended in the major software development workflows resulted in an excessive allocation of resources (time or effort) to accomplish integration and test. Successfully completed projects consumed 40% of their effort in these activities; the percentage was even higher for unsuccessful projects. The overriding reason was that the effort associated with the late scrap and rework of design flaws was collected and implemented during the integration and test phases. Integration is a non-value-added activity, and most integration and test organizations spent 60% of their time integrating—that is, getting the software to work by resolving the design flaws and the frequent scrap and rework associated with these resolutions. It is preferable for integration to be automated, so it will take little time and little effort and enable the integration and test team to focus on demonstrating and testing the software, which are value-added efforts.

ATTACKING SIGNIFICANT RISKS EARLY

Using an iterative development process, the software development team produces the architecture first, allowing integration to occur as the "verification" activity of the design work and allowing design flaws to be detected and resolved earlier in the lifecycle. This replaces the big-bang integration at the end of a project with continuous integration throughout the project. Getting the architecturally important things to be well understood and stable before worrying about the complete breadth and depth of the artifacts should result in scrap and rework rates that decrease or remain stable over the project lifecycle.

The architecture-first approach forces integration into the design phase and demonstrations provide the forcing function for progress. The demonstrations do not eliminate the design breakage; they just make it happen in the design phase where it can be fixed correctly. In an iterative process, the system is "grown" from an immature prototype to a *skeletal* baseline architecture, to increments of useful capabilities (usually implemented scenarios) to, finally, complete product releases. The late-lifecycle integration nightmare is avoided, and a more robust and maintainable solution is produced.

Major milestones provide very tangible results. Designs are now guilty until proven innocent: The project does not move forward until the objectives of the demonstration have been achieved. Results of the demonstration and major milestones contribute to an understanding of the tradeoffs among the requirements, design, plans, technology, and other factors. Based on this understanding, changes to stakeholder expectations can still be renegotiated.

The early phases of the iterative lifecycle (Inception and Elaboration) focus on confronting and resolving, respectively, the business and technical risks before making the big resource commitments required in later phases. Managers of conventional projects tend to do the easy stuff first, thereby demonstrating early progress. A modern process, as shown in Figure 5.2, needs to attack the architecturally significant stuff first, the important 20% of the requirements: use cases, components, and risks.

The "80/20" lessons learned during the past 30 years of software management experience provide a useful perspective for identifying some of the key features of an iterative development philosophy.

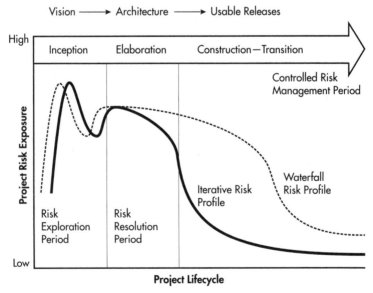

FIGURE 5.2 Architecture first, then production

- *80% of the engineering is consumed by 20% of the require-ments.*
  Do not strive prematurely for high fidelity and full traceability of the complete requirements set. Instead, strive to understand the driving requirements completely before committing resources to full-scale development.

- *80% of the software cost is consumed by 20% of the components.*
  Elaborate the cost-critical components first so that planning and control of cost drivers are well understood early in the lifecycle.

- *80% of the errors are caused by 20% of the components.*
  Elaborate the reliability-critical components first so that assessment activities have enough time to achieve the necessary level of maturity.

- *80% of software scrap and rework is caused by 20% of the changes.*
  Elaborate the change-critical components first so that broad-impact changes occur when the project is nimble.

- *80% of the resource consumption (execution time, disk space, memory) is consumed by 20% of the components.*
  Elaborate the performance-critical components first so that engineering tradeoffs with reliability, changeability, and cost effectiveness can be resolved as early in the lifecycle as possible.

- *80% of the progress is made by 20% of the people.*
  Make sure the initial team that plans the project and designs the architecture is of the highest quality. An adequate plan and adequate architecture can then succeed with an average construction team. An inadequate plan or inadequate architecture will probably not succeed, even with an expert construction team.

IMPROVE PRACTICES INCREMENTALLY TO MEET GOALS

Most teams have some areas of weakness in their practices, but almost none need to change everything they do. Even in cases where they might benefit from significant changes in their practices, it is impractical or impossible to change everything at once. An analysis of team performance usually identifies a set of practices that need improvement. Process frameworks such as the Rational Unified Process and related adoption frameworks such as the Essential Unified Process distill experiences in a variety of typical problem areas. Based on a health check, a plan for improvement can be formed and the practices can be progressively improved over time.

One way to view the impact of improving practices on the economics of software projects is through the differences in resource expenditure profiles between conventional projects and modern iterative projects.

Conventional principles drove software development activities to overexpend during implementation and integration activities. A healthy iterative process, an architecture-first focus, and incorporation of improved practices should result in less total scrap and rework through relatively more emphasis on the high-value activities of management planning, requirements analysis, and design. This results in a more balanced expenditure of resources across the core workflows of a modern process.

One critical lesson learned from successful iterative development projects is that they start out with a planning profile different from the standard profile of a conventional project. If you plan modern iterative projects with the old waterfall planning profile, the chance of success is significantly diminished. By planning a modern project with a more appropriate resource profile derived from successful iterative projects, there is much more flexibility in optimizing the project performance for improvements in productivity, quality, or cycle time, whichever is the business driver.

During the past decade, we have participated in the software process improvement efforts of numerous companies, including most of the leading software development organizations in the Fortune 500 companies. Typical goals are to achieve a 2X, 3X, or 10X increase in productivity, quality, time to market, or some combination of all three, where X corresponds to how well the organization does now. The funny thing is that most of these organizations have only a coarse grasp on what X is, in objective terms.

Table 5.1 characterizes the impact on project expenditure profiles associated with making about a 3X reduction in scrap and rework. This improvement is the primary goal of transitioning from the conventional waterfall software development process to a modern iterative software development process.

TABLE 5.1 Resource Expenditures

Lifecycle Activity	Conventional	Modern
Management	5%	10%
Requirements	5%	10%
Design	10%	15%
Implementation	30%	25%
Test and Assessment	40%	25%
Deployment	5%	5%
Environment	5%	10%
	100%	100%

Standardizing on a common process is a courageous undertaking for a software organization, and there is a wide spectrum of implementations. We have seen organizations attempt to do less (too little standardization, or none) and more (too much standardization) with little success in improving software return on investment. Process standardization requires a very balanced approach.

SUMMARY

The primary goal of process improvement must be improving results while minimizing the overhead associated with nonproductive activities. A results-driven process moves a project forward in visible ways, iteration by iteration. The specific process used may depend on a number of variables, including those under discussion in Part II of this book: Besides process itself, those variables are project complexity, team efficiency, and software tools used. Regardless of the type of process, however, the most important characteristics of process improvement are

- *Using an iterative process.* This means starting small, achieving results, testing as you go, and building required functionality as you go so that the system under development remains integrated throughout the project lifecycle until completion. By contrast, projects whose various parts are not integrated until late in the lifecycle experience a much greater rate of failure. Even successful projects designed and developed according to this waterfall approach require 40% of the entire project effort during the late integration and test phase. (Here's an analogy: Imagine creating a large snowball by designing four or five big chunks of snow you must somehow fit together. It's easier to start small, and grow over time.)
- *Attacking the significant risks first.* By addressing the most critical elements of a system first, the project's design phase can be validated and major flaws can be revealed and remedied. Adding less significant design elements over time becomes less risky.
- *Improving the team's software engineering practices over time.* The various disciplines of iterative development—requirements management, visual modeling, change management, quality management, build and release management, etc.—can present an overwhelming array of new concepts and

techniques for teams accustomed to traditional waterfall-style practices. Even in cases where they might benefit from significant changes in their practices, it is impractical or impossible to change everything at once. It may be most productive to begin process improvement by addressing one set of practices (testing practices, for example), then building team proficiency over time by addressing more disciplines. In addition, project managers should adjust overall resource allocation over the course of the lifecycle according to the conventional versus modern differences shown in Table 5.1.

This brings us to the topic of the next chapter, where we present more concepts for improving team proficiency.

6
. . .
IMPROVING TEAM PROFICIENCY

Getting more done with fewer people is the paramount underlying need for improving software economics. The demand for competent software professionals continues to outpace the supply of qualified individuals. In almost every successful software development project and software organization we have encountered, there is a strong commitment to configuring the smallest, most capable team.

By contrast, most troubled projects are staffed with more people than they require. "Obese" projects usually occur because the project culture is more focused on following a process or over-specializing on skills using a rigid set of roles rather than achieving results. Successful teams focus instead on achieving results, and relax formal roles and rigid processes as needed to achieve those results. This is a subtle but essential difference between successful, results-driven, iterative development projects and unsuccessful process-and-role-driven projects.

So how can organizations use smaller, more capable teams? We have identified three different aspects that need to be addressed: enhancing individual performance, improving project teamwork, and advancing organizational capability.

ENHANCING INDIVIDUAL PERFORMANCE

Organizations that analyze how to improve their employees' proficiency generally focus on only one dimension: training. Although training is an important mechanism for enhancing individual skills, team composition and experience are equally important dimensions that should be considered.

Balance and coverage are two important characteristics of excellent teams. Balance requires leaders and followers, visionaries and crank-turners, optimists and pessimists, conservatives and risk takers. Whenever a team is out of balance, it is vulnerable. It may sound like a cliché, but it's still true: Software development is a team sport. A team loaded with superstars, each striving to set individual records and be the team leader, can be embarrassed by a balanced team of solid players with a few leaders focused on the team result of winning the game. Managers must nurture a culture of teamwork and results rather than individual accomplishment. The other important characteristic, coverage, requires a complement of skill sets that span the breadth of the techniques, tools, and technologies.

In addition, experience counts. Unprecedented systems are much riskier endeavors than systems that have been built before. Experience of the team in building similar systems is one of the most significant predictors of success. This precedent experience is the foundation for differentiating the 20% of the stuff that is architecturally significant in a new system. No matter the maturity of the organization, if team members have never encountered the problem before, they will be learning as they go and their performance will be less than it would be in familiar territory.

IMPROVING PROJECT TEAMWORK

Although it is difficult to make sweeping generalizations about project organizations, some recurring patterns in successful projects suggest that every successful team exhibits the active participation of people with four distinct skill sets: management, architecture, development, and assessment. The project management skills require active participation and typically are supplied by individuals responsible for producing as well as managing—that is, project management is not a spectator sport and passive management and tracking of the project is not effective at producing results. The architecture skills are needed to produce design artifacts and for the integration of components. The development skills are needed for component construction and maintenance activities. The assessment skills are separated from development skills to foster an independent quality perspective as well as to focus on testability and product evaluation activities concurrent with ongoing development throughout the lifecycle. This is not to say that quality tasks are performed by people outside the team because quality is everyone's job, integrated into all activities and checkpoints. However, each team takes responsibility for a different quality perspective.

Some proven practices for building good software architectures are equally valid for building good software organizations. The organization of any project represents the architecture of the team and needs to evolve in synch with the project plans. Defining an explicit architecture team with ownership of architectural issues and integration concerns can provide simpler and less error-prone communications among project teams.

Figure 6.1 illustrates how project team skills needs evolve over the lifecycle of a software development project. Those needs are elaborated on a bit further in the following list:

- **Inception.** *Principally exercises* management skills, especially planning, with enough representation of other skills to ensure that the plans represent a consensus of all perspectives.
- **Elaboration.** *Principally exercises* architectural skills to define, evaluate, and evolve the software architecture. Other

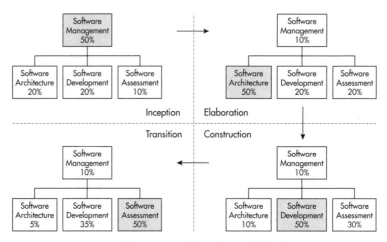

FIGURE 6.1 Team evolution over the software lifecycle

skills exercised include software development and software assessment to achieve a stable architecture baseline.

- **Construction.** *Principally exercises* skills in software development and software assessment.
- **Transition.** *Principally exercises* deployment skills, as well as organizational and logistical skills, in handling usage feedback to drive the organizational and technical deployment activities.

Effective teamwork is much more important than the sum of individual skills and efforts. Project managers need to configure balanced teams with a foundation of solid talent and put highly skilled people in the high-leverage positions. These are some project team management maxims:

- A well-managed project can succeed with average engineering skills.
- An expert team of engineers will almost never succeed if a project is mismanaged.

- A well-architected system can be built by a team of software builders with average skills.
- A poorly architected system will flounder even with an expert team of builders.

ADVANCING ORGANIZATIONAL CAPABILITY

Organizational capability is best measured by trends in project performance rather than by key process area checklists, process audits, and so forth. Figure 6.2 provides some simple graphs of project performance over time to illustrate the expectation for four different levels of organizational capability.

1. **Random.** Immature organizations use ad hoc processes, methods, and tools on each new project. This results in random performance that is frequently unacceptable. Probably 60% of the industry's software organizations still operate with random, unpredictable performance.

2. **Repeatable.** Organizations that are more mature use foundation capabilities roughly traceable to industry best practices. They can achieve repeatable performance with some relatively constant return on investments in processes, methods, training, and tools. In our experience, about 30% of the industry's software development organizations have achieved repeatable project performance.

3. **Improving.** The industry's better software organizations achieve common process frameworks, methods, training, and tools across an organization within a common line of business. Consistent, objective metrics can be used across projects, which can result in an improving return on investment from project to project. This is the underlying goal of ISO 9000 or SEWE CMM process-improvement initiatives, although most such initiatives tend to take

process- and activity-focused perspectives rather than pro-
ject-result-focused perspectives. At most, 10% of the industry's software development organizations operate today at
this level of capability.

4. **Market-leading.** Organizations achieve excellent capability,
which should align with market leadership, when they have
executed multiple projects under a common framework
with successively better performance. Market leaders have
achieved an objective experience base from which they can
optimize business performance across multiple performance
dimensions (trading off quality, time-to-market, and costs);
and practice quantitative process management.

In any engineering venture, where intellectual property is the
real product, the dominant productivity factors will be staff skills, teamwork, and motivation. To the extent possible, effective staffing will
focus on engaging high-leverage people early in an iteratively managed project, when the team is relatively small. The later production

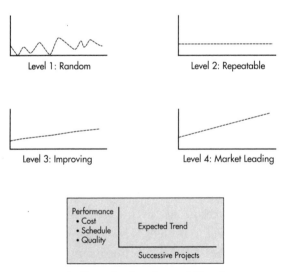

FIGURE 6.2 Organizational capability improvement measured through
successive project performance

phases, when teams are typically much larger, should then operate with far less dependency on scarce expertise.

SUMMARY

Enhancing individual performance, improving project teamwork, and advancing organizational capability are three important goals toward achieving greater overall team proficiency. An underlying principle here is the strength of smaller, more capable teams focused on results rather than adherence to a process.

Enhancing individual performance doesn't mean concentrated effort on an individual's strengths, but rather understanding the ways in which an individual's strengths can be amplified when, as a team player, he or she finds the right niche within a team. Software development is a team sport, and no team can succeed if everyone is a superstar striving to set records and be the team leader. Managers must nurture a culture of teamwork and results, which means finding the best role for each individual talent.

Improving project teamwork requires people with four distinct skill sets: management, architecture, development, and assessment. Project management requires active participation by individuals responsible for producing as well as managing; project management is not a spectator sport and passive management does not produce results. Architecture skills are needed to produce design artifacts and for the integration of components. Development skills are needed for component construction and maintenance activities. Assessment skills are separated from development skills to foster an independent quality perspective as well as to focus on testability and product evaluation activities concurrent with ongoing development throughout the lifecycle.

Finally, incremental advances in organizational capability are a truer measure of team proficiency and project performance than checklists and process audits can reveal. A team that is steadily improving over time will progress through four phases of capability maturity: from 1) random and immature, where ad hoc processes, methods, and tools are brought to bear on each new project; to 2) repeatable, where organizations achieve relatively constant return on investments in processes, methods, training, and tools; to 3) improving, where common process frameworks, methods, training, etc. can be used across projects with improved return on investment from project to project; to 4) market-leading, where organizations have executed multiple projects under a common framework from which they can optimize business performance across multiple dimensions.

7
. . .

IMPROVING AUTOMATION THROUGH INTEGRATED TOOLS

In an earlier chapter, we described process improvements associated with transitioning to iterative development. These improvements are focused on eliminating steps and minimizing the scrap and rework that become inevitable in the conventional process. Another form of process improvement is to improve the efficiency of certain steps by adopting or improving automation through integrated tools.

Today's integrated software development environments, combined with service-oriented architectures, visual modeling approaches, and the use of patterns and frameworks, enable many previously manual tasks to be automated. Activities such as analysis of designs, data translations, quality checks, and other tasks involving a deterministic production of artifacts can now be done with minimal human intervention. Specialized tools that can typically benefit modern software development approaches include tools for requirements management, visual modeling, document automation, host/target programming tools, automated regression testing, integrated change management, build automation, and feature/defect tracking.

Today, most software organizations face the need to integrate their own environment and infrastructure for software development. This typically results in the selection of more or less incompatible tools with different information repositories—from different vendors, on different platforms, using different jargon, and based on different process assumptions. Integrating and maintaining such an infrastructure has proved to be much more problematic than expected.

An important enabler of a modern approach is appropriate tooling to automate and instrument key aspects of the development effort. Commercial processes, methods, and tools have synthesized and packaged industry best practices into mature approaches applicable across the spectrum of software development domains. The return on investment in these commercial environments scales up significantly with the size of the software development organization, promotes useful levels of standardization, and minimizes the additional organizational burden of maintaining proprietary alternatives.

IMPROVING HUMAN PRODUCTIVITY

Planning tools, requirements management tools, visual modeling tools, compilers, editors, debuggers, quality assurance analysis tools, test tools, and user interfaces provide crucial automation support for evolving the intermediate products of a software engineering effort. Moreover, configuration management environments provide the foundation for executing and instrumenting the development effort. Viewed in isolation, tools and automation generally yield 20% to 40% improvements in effort. These same tools and environments, however, are also primary vehicles for reducing complexity and improving process automation, so their impact can be much greater.

Tool automation can help reduce the overall complexity in automated code generation from UML design models, for example.

Designers working at a relatively high level of abstraction in UML may compose a model that includes graphical icons, relationships, and attributes in a few diagrams. Visual modeling tools can capture the diagrams in a persistent representation and automate the creation of a large number of source code statements in a desired programming language. Hundreds of lines of source code are typically generated from tens of human-generated visual modeling elements. This 10-to-1 reduction in the amount of human-generated stuff is one dimension of complexity reduction enabled by visual modeling notations and tools.

ELIMINATING ERROR SOURCES

Each phase of development produces a certain amount of precision in the product/system description called software artifacts. Lifecycle software artifacts are organized into five sets that are roughly partitioned by the underlying language of:

1. Requirements (organized text and UML models of the problem space)
2. Design (UML models of the solution space)
3. Implementation (human-readable programming language and associated source files)
4. Deployment (machine-processable languages and associated files)
5. Management (ad hoc textual formats such as plans, schedules, metrics, and spreadsheets)

At any point in the lifecycle, the different artifact sets should be in balance, at compatible detail levels, and traceable to each other. As development proceeds, each part evolves in more detail. When the system is complete, all five sets are fully elaborated and consistent with each other. As the industry has moved into maintaining different information repositories for the engineering artifacts, we now need automation support to ensure efficient and error-free transition of data from one artifact to another. Round-trip engineering describes the environment support needed to change an artifact freely and have other artifacts automatically changed so that consistency is maintained among the entire set of requirements, design, implementation, and deployment artifacts.

ENABLING PROCESS IMPROVEMENTS

Real-world project experience has shown that a highly integrated environment is necessary both to facilitate and to enforce management control of the process. An environment that captures artifacts in structured engineering languages such as UML and programming languages can provide semantic integration (where the environment understands the detailed meaning of the development artifacts) and significant process automation to improve productivity and software quality. An environment that supports incremental compilation, automated system builds, and integrated regression testing can provide rapid turnaround for iterative development, allow development teams to iterate more freely, and accelerate the adoption of modern techniques.

Objective measures are required for assessing the quality of a software product and the progress of the work, which provide different perspectives of a software effort. Architects are more concerned with quality indicators; managers are usually more concerned with progress indicators. The success of any software process whose metrics are collected manually will be limited. The most important software metrics are simple, objective measures of how various perspectives of the product/project are changing. Absolute measures are usually much less important than relative changes with respect to time. The dynamic nature of software projects requires that these measures be available at any time, ideally captured at levels corresponding to the various subsets of the evolving product (subsystem, release, version, component, team), and maintained such that trends can be observed and assessed. Such continuous availability has only been achieved in development/integration environments that enable metrics to be obtained as an automated by-product of the completion of work.

SUMMARY

Today's integrated software development environments enable many previously manual tasks to be automated. Activities such as design analysis, data translations, quality checks, and other tasks involving a deterministic production of artifacts can now be done with minimal human intervention. Specialized tools can handle requirements management, regression testing, change management, build automation, and more. However, the use of multiple software tools to help automate these areas of the development life-cycle needs to be compatible and based on standards to achieve adequate return on investment. The importance of standardized tools grows with the size of the software development organization.

Used effectively, tools and automation can yield 20% to 40% improvements in software engineering effort compared to manual methods. These same tools and environments can also reduce the overall complexity in automated code generation with a 10-to-1 reduction in the amount of human-generated code.

As the engineering artifacts generated over the course of a software development process evolve, automation helps ensure efficient and error-free transition of data from one artifact to another. Changes to one artifact require that other artifacts be automatically changed to maintain consistency throughout all requirements, design, implementation, and deployment artifacts.

An automated tooling environment can provide rapid turnaround for iterative development, and allow development teams to iterate more freely and more rapidly adopt modern techniques.

Metrics are critical for understanding the success in adopting modern engineering practices—including the use of integrated tools. The most important software metrics are simple, objective measures of how various perspectives of the product/project are changing, and these measures can most easily be obtained as output from the automated tool environment.

Much more on metrics gathering and analysis will be provided in Part III.

8

. . .

ACCELERATING CULTURE CHANGE
THROUGH COMMON SENSE

As discussed in Part I of this book, the track record has been that three out of four projects don't succeed. Project managers and organizations tend to "play defense," which typically results in an overemphasis on a document trail to support how, in the event of failure, nothing was their fault. In our experience, the organizations that have truly achieved a quantum leap in improving their software economics are the ones that have demonstrated judicious risk management and savvy success management by playing offense, attacking each of the four dimensions—complexity, process, teams, and tools—in an aggressive, yet balanced, fashion.

PROFILES OF SUCCESSFUL ORGANIZATIONS

Figure 8.1 illustrates the target project profiles that result when a software organization attacks all four dimensions of our simplified software economics framework. These organizations execute projects with a profile similar to that of the upper shaded region using a modern iterative process, capable teams supported by an integrated

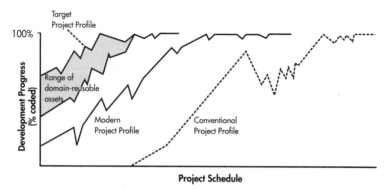

FIGURE 8.1 Target project profiles for organizations pursuing improvements along four dimensions

environment, and a component-based architecture that reduces the complexity of custom development through the use of an architectural pattern with a rich supply of existing components.

Today, roughly 60% of the industry still operates according to the conventional project profile. About 30% has transitioned to the modern project profile. Less than 10% is already achieving improved software economics and experiencing results similar to the target project profile. Organizations that have succeeded are deploying software products that are constructed largely out of existing components in 50% less time, with 50% less development resources, maintained by teams 50% the size of those required by legacy systems.

In making the transition to new techniques and technologies, there is always apprehension and concern about failing. Maintaining the status quo and relying on existing methods is usually considered the safest path. In the software industry, however, where most organizations succeed on only a small percentage of their software projects, maintaining the status quo is not always safe. When an organization does decide to make a transition, two pieces of conventional wisdom are usually offered both by internal champions and by external change agents:

1. Pioneer any new techniques on a small pilot program.
2. Be prepared to spend more resources (money and time) on your first project that makes the transition.

In our experience, both recommendations are counter-productive. The organizations that succeed take the opposite approach: They implement the changes on a business-critical project, and they explicitly plan to demonstrate the business improvements (in resources or time required) on that first critical project.

KEYS TO SUCCESS

Why does the bold approach succeed? Our experience shows that meaningful organizational change depends on A-players and committed middle-level managers. A-players are typically assigned to the front lines, working on business-critical projects. These are the projects that will have the most impact on near-term business. Most organizations cannot afford to assign A-players to noncritical pilot projects.

Middle-level managers are important because they lay out resource plans and schedules. When they propose to improve a process by making a change, and then sell their proposal by giving the change initiative as the reason, it is a sure sign that these leaders (and their teams) believe that a new method, process, technique, or tool will make a difference. On the other hand, if a manager accountable for performance proposes that a project will take more time or need more people because of a new approach, this is usually a sign that the project is incorporating a change that the manager and team only half-heartedly support. The change may have been mandated, or it may have come about because of some line of reasoning the team has not completely bought into. The first team, which believes that a certain change will achieve better results, will usually do whatever it takes to make that claim come true. Ownership by the right people is the key to success. Look for it.

Successful software management is hard work. Technical breakthroughs, process breakthroughs, and new tools will make it easier, but management discipline will continue to be the crux of software project success. New technological advances will be accompanied by new opportunities for software applications, new dimensions of complexity, new avenues of automation, and new customers with different priorities. Accommodating these changes will perturb many of our ingrained software management values and priorities. However, striking a balance among requirements, designs, and plans will remain the underlying objective of future software management endeavors, just as it is today.

Improving software economics is not revolutionary; numerous projects have been practicing some of these techniques for years. However, many of the techniques suggested here will require non-trivial paradigm shifts. It is important to be prepared for these shifts in order to avoid as many sources of friction as possible. Some of these changes will be resisted by certain stakeholders or by certain contingencies within a project or organization. This resistance must be overcome to transition successfully to a modern software management process and supporting methods and tools. In some cases, distinguishing objective opposition from stubborn resistance will present a challenge.

The following sections discuss some rough indicators of a successful transition to a modern culture focused on improved software business performance. These are things to look for in order to differentiate projects and organizations that have made a genuine cultural transition from those that have only put up a façade.

Lower- and Middle-Level Managers Are the Key Performers

Hands-on management skills vary, but competent first-line managers typically spend much of their time performing, especially focused on understanding the status of the project first hand and developing plans and estimates. Above all, the person managing an effort ought to plan it. This does not mean approving the plan; it means participating in its development. In independent project assessments we have performed, a good indicator of trouble ahead is a manager who did not author the plan or take ownership in it. The stakeholders affected by this transition are software project managers and team leaders.

Requirements, Designs, and Plans Are Fluid and Tangible

The conventional software development process focuses too much on producing documents that attempt to describe the software product and too little on producing tangible increments of the products themselves. Major milestones are defined solely in terms of specific documents. Development organizations are driven to produce tons of paper to meet milestones rather than expend their energy on tasks that will reduce risk and produce quality software. An iterative process requires actual construction of a sequence of progressively more complete systems that demonstrate the architecture, enable objective requirements negotiations, validate the technical approach, and address resolution of key risks. Ideally, all stakeholders focus on these real milestones, with incremental deliveries of useful functionality and commensurate increases in objective understanding of the tradeoffs among requirements, designs, and plans rather than speculative paper descriptions of the end-item vision. The transition to a less document-driven environment will be embraced by the engineering teams; it will probably be resisted by traditional product and project monitors.

Ambitious Demonstrations Are Encouraged

The purpose of early lifecycle demonstrations is to expose design flaws, not to put up a façade. Stakeholders should not overreact to early mistakes, digressions, or immature designs. Evaluation criteria in early release plans are coarse goals, not requirements. If early

engineering obstacles are overemphasized, development organizations will set up future iterations to be less ambitious. On the other
hand, stakeholders should not tolerate lack of follow-through in
resolving issues. If negative trends are not addressed with vigor, they
can cause serious perturbations later on. Open and attentive follow-
through is necessary to resolve issues. The management team is
most likely to resist these demonstrations (especially if the project
was oversold) because they will expose any engineering or process
issues that were easy to hide using the conventional process.
Customers, users, and the engineering team will embrace them for
exactly the same reason.

Good and Bad Project Performance Is Much More Obvious Earlier in the Lifecycle

Real-world project experience has shown time and again that it is
the early phases that make or break a project. It is therefore of paramount importance to have absolutely the right start-up team for the
early planning and architecture activities. If these early phases are
done right with good teams, projects can be completed successfully
with nominal teams evolving the applications into the final product.
If the planning and architecture work is not performed adequately,
however, all the expert programmers and testers in the world will
probably not make the project successful. No one should resist early
staffing with the right team. Most organizations, however, have
scarce resources for early lifecycle roles and are hesitant to make the
necessary staff allocations.

Early Iterations Will Be Immature

External stakeholders, including customers and users, cannot
expect initial deliveries to perform up to specification, to be complete, to be fully reliable, or to have end-target levels of quality or
performance. On the other hand, development organizations must

be held accountable for, and demonstrate, tangible improvements and positive trends in successive increments. These trends usually indicate convergence toward specifications. Objectively quantifying changes, fixes, and upgrades will help all stakeholders evaluate the quality of the process and environment for future activities. Objective insight into performance issues occurs early in the lifecycle in almost every successful project. This is a sign of an immature design but a mature design process. All stakeholders will initially be concerned over early performance issues. Development engineers will embrace the emphasis on early demonstrations and the ability to assess and evaluate performance tradeoffs in subsequent releases. Although customers and users may have difficulty accepting the flaws of early releases, they should be impressed by later increments. The development team will accept immaturity as a natural part of the process.

Detailed and Complete Artifacts Are Less Important Early, More Important Later

It is a waste of time to worry about the details (traceability, thoroughness, and completeness) of the artifact sets until a baseline is achieved that is useful enough and stable enough to warrant time-consuming analyses of these quality factors. Project leaders should avoid squandering early engineering cycles and precious resources on adding content and quality precision to artifacts that may quickly become obsolete. Although the development team will embrace the transition to this approach wholeheartedly, traditional contract monitors will resist the early de-emphasis on completeness.

Real Issues Surface and Get Resolved Systematically

Successful projects recognize that requirements and designs evolve together through a process of continuous negotiation, tradeoff, and bartering toward best value; they do not blindly adhere to a set of ambiguous contract clauses or requirements statements. On a healthy project that is making progress, it should be easy to differentiate between real and apparent issues.

Quality Assurance Is Everyone's Job, Not a Separate Discipline

Many organizations have a separate group called Quality Assurance. We are generally against the concept of separate quality assurance activities, teams, or artifacts. Quality assurance should be woven into every role, every activity, and every artifact. True quality assurance is measured by tangible progress and objective data, not by checklists, meetings, and inspections. The software project manager or delegate should assume the role of ensuring that quality assurance is properly woven into the process. The traditional policing by a separate team of inspectors should be replaced by the self-policing teamwork of an organization with a mature process, common objectives, and common incentives. Traditional managers and quality assurance personnel will resist this transition, but engineering teams will embrace it.

Investments in Automation Are Viewed as Necessary

Because iterative development projects require extensive automation, it is important not to underinvest in the capital environment. It is also important for stakeholders to acquire an integrated environment that permits efficient participation in an iterative development. Without this, interactions with the development organization will degenerate to paper exchanges and many of the issues of the traditional process. These investments may be opposed by organization managers overly focused on near-term financial results or project personnel who favor a narrow project focus over a global solution that serves both the project and the organization's goals.

RECOMMENDATION: SELECT THE RIGHT PROJECT, THE RIGHT PEOPLE, AND THE RIGHT GOALS

In our experience, the most successful organizational paradigm shifts resulted from similar sets of circumstances. These organizations took their most critical project and highest caliber personnel, gave them adequate resources, and demanded better results. If an organization expects a new method, tool, or technology to have an adverse impact on the results of the trailblazing project, that expectation is almost certain to come true. Why? Because no organization manager would knowingly cause an adverse impact on the most important projects in an organization, to which the best people are assigned. Therefore, the trailblazing project will be a noncritical project, staffed with noncritical personnel of whom less is expected. The expectation of an adverse impact ends up being a self-fulfilling prophecy.

The best way to transition to improved software economics is to take the following shot:

- **Ready.** Understand modern processes, approaches, and technologies. Define (or improve, or optimize) your process to support iterative development in the context of your business priorities. Support the process with mature environments, tools, architectural patterns, and components.
- **Aim.** Select a project critical to the organization's business. Staff it with the right team of complementary resources.
- **Fire.** Execute the organizational and project-level plans with vigor and follow-through.

SUMMARY

The most successful software development organizations, compared to other teams, are deploying software products constructed largely out of existing components in 50% less time, with 50% less development resources, and maintained by teams 50% the size of those required by legacy systems. Moreover, these organizations have implemented changes to their development processes, teams, and tools in the context of a business-critical project (rather than safe, noncritical pilot projects), and they can demonstrate real business improvements as a result. This may seem counterintuitive; the approach works because critical business projects—and the meaningful organizational change that enables their success—depend on A-players and committed middle-level managers assigned to the front lines. Most organizations cannot afford to assign A-players to noncritical pilot projects.

Successful transition to a modern software development culture must be focused on improved software business performance. Here are the key points to understand in making that transition:

- Lower- and middle-level managers are the key performers.
- Requirements, designs, and plans are fluid and tangible.
- Ambitious demonstrations are encouraged.
- Good and bad project performance is much more obvious earlier in the lifecycle.
- Early iterations will be immature.
- Detailed and complete artifacts are less important early, more important later.
- Real issues—the serious ones, not just the apparent ones— surface and get resolved systematically.
- Quality assurance is everyone's job, not a separate discipline.
- Investments in automation are viewed as necessary.

When all the buzzwords and cosmetics are stripped away, most of our advice boils down to simple common sense: Successful organizations take their most critical project and highest caliber personnel, give them adequate resources, and demand better results.

In this part of the book, we have presented key lessons about improving software economics that we have learned through 20 years of working in the trenches with thousands of customers. In Part III, we will take this common sense a step further by describing how to measure the improvements that iterative, incremental software development techniques can make within your organization.

PART III
PRACTICAL MEASUREMENT FOR SOFTWARE ENGINEERING

Most organizations use measurements in various ways to assess perfor-mance or effectiveness of different courses of action. Without measure-ment, they have little more than subjective observation to determine whether things are on track; measurement is inevitable. But measure-ment is a tricky thing—many times you cannot directly measure what you really want to know about, as in cases where you measure increases in output (productivity) when you really would like to know about effectiveness of resource utilization.

There is a more subtle aspect to measurement: People pay atten-tion to things being measured, and assume those measured things are important. Even when measurements are not directly tied to rewards, people will work to improve their performance in areas where they per-ceive they are being measured. Perception is key. Sometimes, man-agers overtly say one thing and reinforce something else through measurements, which effectively undermines their stated objectives.

9

· · ·

A PRACTICAL VIEW OF SOFTWARE
DEVELOPMENT METRICS

Measurement implies that the thing being measured is meaningful, and the software development team looks to those measurements for cues about what is important. Software developers interpret this information, and often change their behavior to deliver what they think the people directing the measurement want.

This effect shows itself in a number of ways—from telling managers what they think they want to hear when asked, "How is the project going?" to reporting sometimes more, sometimes fewer, hours than were actually worked, depending on whether they think working more hours than expected is a good thing (often the sign of a "hero culture") or a bad thing (working extra hours is often the sign of a project in trouble).

The best way to counter the unintended consequences of measurement is to be completely transparent about what you are measuring and why, which requires you to be completely transparent about project goals and how measurements relate to project goals.

MEASUREMENTS AND GOALS

Before you decide what to measure, you need to decide what you want to achieve. Most organizations focus on goals that fall into three broad areas:

- Reducing the time it takes to deliver a solution (time to market), subject to a minimum level of functionality, and a given level of quality and cost.
- Reducing cost, subject to a minimum level of functionality, and a given level of quality and usually constraints on time to market.
- Improving quality, subject to constraints on a minimum level of functionality, and on cost and time to market.

The essence of management is to manage these trade offs in an acceptable way to achieve the desired result. To do so, targets need to be set for these four areas—that is, cost, time, scope, and quality. Most projects measure cost and time, but scope and quality affect cost and time and need to be measured as well. In fact, most measures of project success must include more than cost and time—the delivered solution needs to do something useful (scope) and must do so with acceptable quality.

VARIABILITY AND GOALS

Prediction is very difficult, especially if it's about the future.
—Niels Bohr

A goal is a kind of prediction—a statement about what will constitute success at some point in the future. Reality may fall short of the goal or, if you're lucky, it may exceed the goal. In statistical terms, project results are random variables, and goals are estimates of desired values for those random variables.

When considering random variables, remember that actual observations are centered around an average, or *mean* value. The

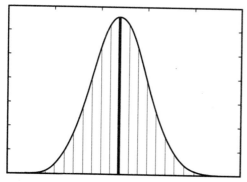

FIGURE 9.1 Normal probability density function, which illustrates that actual observations may vary from the expected (or average)

spread of the distribution, called its *variability*, indicates the degree to which observed values will vary from the mean. In a symmetrical distribution, values are equally likely to fall above the mean as below it, and the most likely value, the *mode*, is equal to the mean. Figure 9.1 shows a typical normal probability density function, so called because most observations fall into this sort of distribution.

One of the key mistakes that people make is specifying only one number for a goal—the expected value (or mean value) to be achieved. But reality is variable, and to take this into account, we need to establish tolerances for goals, within which performance is considered acceptable. Doing so is a useful exercise, because it forces you to consider the amount of variability you will accept, and it will prevent unnecessary focus on minimizing irrelevant variability while maintaining focus on important variance.

MEASUREMENT AND ITERATIVE DEVELOPMENT

One of the principal benefits of an iterative approach to software development is that it makes a conscious effort to reduce variance over the course of the project, as shown in Figure 9.2. Note that this

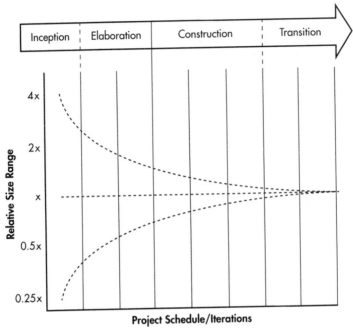

FIGURE 9.2 The iterative development approach reduces variance over the course of a project

illustration turns the sample from Figure 9.1 on its side, achieving a very narrow distribution toward the end of the iterative lifecycle.

The line labeled "x" represents the expected value of an estimate, whereas the dashed lines above and below this line represent the expected variation around these estimates. Over the course of the project, the variation decreases as risks are retired, as shown in Figure 9.3.

Each of the four phases shown in Figure 9.3—Inception, Elaboration, Construction, and Transition—focus on mitigating different types of risks. As a result, the goals for each phase differ as well. This means that the measurements used to track progress toward project goals need to change, phase by phase.

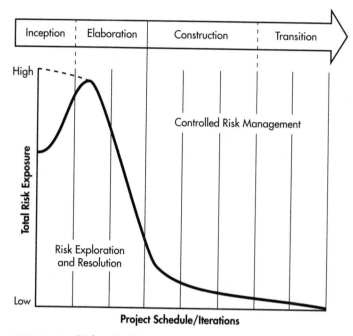

FIGURE 9.3 Risk, which greatly contributes to variance and unpredictability, is reduced over time in an iterative project

WHEN MEASUREMENT GOES WRONG

Among the absolute worst practices followed by many organizations is "planning in detail up front, then measuring to plan." Planning and measurement, by themselves, are not bad things, but the timing employed by most organizations actually does more to encourage wrong behavior than any other single practice. Here's what normally happens:

1. A project is initiated, and as one of the earliest actions a project manager creates a project plan. Based on sketchy information about the problems to be solved and vague goals, the project manager does his or her best to "guess" what the schedule and costs will look like.

2. No matter how many *caveats* are put forth about the tentative nature of the plan, the plan takes on a life of its own. Managers higher in the organization lose sight of the fact that early plans are really just thought experiments—they are no more valid than the assumptions on which they are based. The plan becomes a kind of *prediction* about what success will look like, and the focus of management oversight shifts to measuring deviations from plan, rather than on steering the project toward a successful outcome. The plan becomes an albatross around the neck of the project manager.

3. Project team members are discouraged from taking actions that are not in accordance with the plan, even when everyone seems to know that the plan is a complete fiction, disconnected from the daily realities of the project. Although the plan could, in theory, be correct, it is very unlikely that it will be. When it inevitably fails to perfectly anticipate the future, unquestioningly following the project plan often leads to failure.

4. When the plan fails to match reality, the only logical course is to deviate from the plan; but if the management system punishes deviations from plan, it often leaves team members with no option but to create the illusion that they are following the plan, even when they are not. This sort of behavior does no one any good.

Why does this sort of thing happen? The problem is not planning per se, but rather planning in the absence of reality and in opposition to experience. The problem is planning in detail things that cannot be planned at all, because not enough is known, and then holding the team "accountable" for adherence to the fabrication.

A better approach is to understand where the project needs to end up, and then to use flexibility in steering toward that goal *continuously* throughout the entire project. To do this, you need to be looking for the right information at different points in the project.

WHAT'S WRONG WITH DETAILED
UP-FRONT PLANNING?

Although the preceding discussion touches upon what is wrong with planning in detail at the project outset, the practice is so pervasive and such a part of the project management tradition that it needs special attention to discourage its use. Briefly, creating and managing to a detailed plan early in the project is wrong because

- It is unrealistic to expect that a project manager should be capable of the technical depth necessary to determine project activities and their timing for the technical work on the project. Milestones and goals can be determined, but the actual work that will be needed to reach those goals is beyond the technical understanding of the average project manager. The technical expertise needed to plan at any meaningful level of precision requires the involvement of the larger development team, and any "planning" done by the project manager is likely to be speculative at best.
- The uncertainty of specific courses of action early in the project is sufficiently high that even detailed plans created by the development team are speculative. The early days and weeks of the project are characterized by lack of reliable information about what problems need to be solved and what goals need to be achieved; detailed planning in light of this lack of information is simply a waste of time.
- If early detailed planning is a waste of time, measuring to a detailed plan created early in the project is dangerous and often dooms the project to fail. Holding people accountable for flawed and faulty plans discourages people from taking the right actions when information becomes available. It can also force people to take the wrong actions because the plan tells them to do so; or more often, it encourages them to create "two sets of books"—one for the "real" project work and one that tracks back to the original but flawed

plan against which they are being measured. Either way, the early detailed plan encourages the wrong behavior.

So, if measuring the project against a detailed project plan is not the right approach, what should be measured to ensure that a project is on track?

DECIDING WHAT TO MEASURE, PHASE BY PHASE

Because each phase of a project deals with different challenges, you need to measure different things at different points in the project. For illustration purposes, we will use the four phases of the Unified Process (Inception, Elaboration, Construction, and Transition), each of which focuses on a different set of goals pertaining to its different associated risks—that is, each phase focuses on mitigating a different set of risks.

But before we get to a discussion of risk, it's important to revisit the broad goals we described earlier in this book for each of the phases, as shown in Figure 9.4.

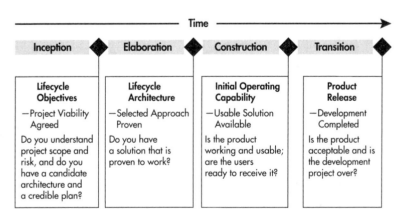

FIGURE 9.4 Goals and objectives associated with each of the four lifecycle phases

SUMMARY

Before you decide what to measure, be certain that you understand the goals. Metrics taken simply because the numbers are readily available—metrics for the sake of metrics—seldom contribute to the goal and can often reinforce the wrong behavior. The best way to counter the unintended consequences of measurement is to be completely transparent about what you are measuring and why.

One of the principal benefits of an iterative approach to software development is that it makes a conscious effort to reduce variance over the course of the project. In healthy projects, risks are retired over time, the variance grows smaller, and the project progresses toward a successful conclusion. In unhealthy projects, the plan becomes a kind of prediction about what success will look like, and management focus shifts to measuring deviations from plan rather than on steering the project toward a successful outcome. And if the management system punishes deviations from plan, the team has no option but to create the *illusion* that they are following the plan, which does no one any good.

To put it simply, creating and managing to a detailed plan early in the project is wrong. Milestones and goals can be determined, but the actual work needed to reach those goals is beyond the technical understanding of the project manager. Detailed plans created by the development team early on are speculative, and measuring to a detailed plan created early in the project is dangerous and often dooms the project to failure.

A better approach is to understand where the project needs to end up, and then to use flexibility in steering toward that goal continuously throughout the entire project. The appropriate metrics change, phase by phase. Each of the four phases of the Unified Process— Inception, Elaboration, Construction, and Transition—focuses on a different set of goals pertaining to its different associated risks.

In the remaining chapters, we will describe how to establish measurements appropriate to each of the four process phases, to determine if the project is on track to achieving these goals.

10

· · ·

WHAT TO MEASURE IN THE
INCEPTION PHASE

The Inception phase has the following goals:

- To identify and mitigate business, project, and funding risks
- To assess the viability of the project, both technically and financially
- To agree to the scope and objectives of the project
- To form an overall plan for moving ahead

Every project needs to be funded for at least the Inception phase; funding for subsequent phases will depend on the outcome of the Inception phase.

The focus of the Inception phase is on mitigating the risk that the project might be either economically undesirable or technically infeasible. For this, the team must explore the benefits and costs of the project so that a firm decision can be made about whether to proceed. At the end of the Inception phase, the stakeholders agree that the project is feasible and that the business case for the project is achievable if the project proceeds as planned. Everyone must agree that the project is viable—that is, that the project is worth doing and the time and cost estimates are credible. If these things *cannot* be settled, it is best to forego the project and turn your attention to more worthy projects.

Measurement in this phase is focused on answering the following questions:

- What is the business benefit of the project?
- What is the expected cost to deliver the business benefit?
- Is the project worth completing?

The first two questions are the most difficult, as their answers dictate the answer to the third question. In the next two sections, we will discuss how to measure the business benefit and expected cost, and how to factor these answers into an overall measurement plan.

ASSESSING FINANCIAL VIABILITY

The expected business benefit establishes constraints on what the business is willing to spend to obtain those benefits. At this phase of the project, precise estimates are not needed; rough estimates should be sufficient to establish that there is clear value in pursuing the project.

Business benefits are usually expressed in terms of *net present value (NPV)*, which takes into account the time-value of money obtained, as well as risk. Mathematically, it is defined as shown in Figure 10.1.

$$NPV = \text{initial investment} + \sum_{t=1}^{t = \text{end of project}} \frac{(\text{Cash Flows at Year } t)}{(1 + r)^t}$$

FIGURE 10.1 Net present value

The *end of the project* is really the lifespan of the solution, and *r* is the *required rate of return*, of the project. Some attention should be given to choosing the *required rate of return* to make sure that it adequately accounts for the risk of the project. Typically, the required rate of return is based on projects of equivalent risk.

Ignoring the initial investment (covered in the next section under Project Cost), the business benefits are estimated by the future cash flows arising from the solution—both the positive ones related to increased revenues as well as negative cash flows resulting from expected maintenance.

Supporting evidence for the business benefit estimates usually includes market research data for new products or services, business cost data for projects focused on cost reduction, or both. As the NPV formula implies, the specific timing of the estimates is important: Benefits received sooner are much more valuable than benefits received in the future.

The benefits for projects driven by compliance regulations are easier to estimate. The project benefit is estimated by the penalty avoidance. The timing of the benefits of compliance is still important, however.

ASSESSING TECHNICAL VIABILITY AND ESTIMATING OVERALL PROJECT COST

Obtaining estimates on the expected cost can, in theory, be obtained from parametric estimation models based on historical cost data, but the scarcity of available data relevant to the project at hand usually means that you must build some small but representative part of the system in order to extrapolate project cost and schedule data. It helps to choose a few representative scenarios and develop the software to deliver them. Doing this usually confirms whether your assumptions about the project's technical complexity are correct, even if you have to "stub out" a fair amount of the system functionality. Even if you have parametric estimation models, the early prototyping effort helps you to validate the parametric estimates.

From this early prototyping effort, two main results emerge: a qualitative assessment of whether the project is technically feasible, and quantitative measures of project schedule and cost. The raw data obtained from the early prototyping is typically fed into one or more estimation models to derive cost information. Using more than one model is a useful way to cross-validate estimates—wide differences in predictions provided by the models are a signal that you should analyze your assumptions more carefully.

In Chapter 9, Figure 9.3 presented an expected risk curve for the project, with risks peaking in the early Elaboration phase and declining afterward. In fact, the curve shown in Figure 9.3 is the *ideal* risk profile that you should strive for, one that you will achieve if you are actively and aggressively managing risk. There is nothing magical about the mere passage of time that causes risks to decline in number and severity. In order to bring risks under control, you need to have a sense of what risks you face and when you expect to mitigate them. Many projects collect a risk list; most frequently, they do this early in the project, but they fail to use the list as a key management tool. It is not enough to simply collect a risk list; you also need to map the risks onto iterations in an overall project plan and then later plan activities that will mitigate the risks assigned to the iteration as you plan that iteration. In the early mapping of risks to iterations, you don't need to create a detailed plan of project activities; just mapping risks to iterations is good enough at this stage. Doing so gives you a sense of whether you are addressing risks early enough. As you assign the risks to iterations, make sure to assign big risks to early iterations, which means that some exploration is required in the Inception phase to understand what risks you may face.

Mapping these risks and making some educated guesses about what work will be needed to address them gives you a sense of what resources will be required, by iteration. Again, the goal is not to create a detailed plan, but to provide a general roadmap for project staffing. This staffing model (or *map* if the word *model* sounds too formal) provides input to the overall cost estimate by establishing timing for the costs.

ITERATION IN THE INCEPTION PHASE

Sometimes it takes more than one iteration to determine the business viability of the project. This usually happens because of unexpected difficulty in determining the project's technical or financial viability. Extending the previous discussion of risk, it sometimes takes more than one iteration to mitigate the business risks associated with the project.

Usually, the Inception phase is *time-boxed*, meaning that a predetermined amount of time, usually a month, is given to the phase. Normally, the Inception phase has only a single iteration—at the beginning of the project, there is usually no reason to assume otherwise. As the iteration progresses and nears the end, the results are sometimes sufficiently inconclusive to warrant further exploration, but not so conclusive to dictate abandoning the project. As a result, an additional iteration is funded to conclude the investigation.

Many of us have had experiences with employers who used a process that had as its first phase a "feasibility study." The Inception phase serves this purpose but with a twist: It is typically essential to do some prototyping to explore the technical feasibility of the project, whereas the old feasibility study was often a largely theoretical undertaking.

Determining financial viability is usually a two-step process. First, there is often a *time to market* factor to consider: Sometimes if a solution cannot be delivered to market within a specific time window, the project is not worth completing. If the time to market requirement can be met, the NPV of the proposed solution is calculated. If the NPV is negative, the project is not worth pursuing.

If the NPV is positive, the project may be worth pursuing, provided that it does not compete for funding with other higher-valued projects.

Factoring risk into goals tends to be subjective and is best accomplished by increasing the variability of the estimates—in effect, by widening the "margin for error." Most estimates in this phase are, in reality, highly subjective and can be off by wide margins. The most valuable question to ask about an estimate is not "Is it accurate?" but "How wide a range of values is possible?" Alternatively, variability in the estimates can be accommodated by increasing the required rate of return for the project in the NPV calculation. Typically, a number of scenarios are analyzed to determine the expected-case and the worst-case values for NPV. Often, the decision to go ahead with a project is based on whether the worst-case NPV is within acceptable limits.

After the solution is deployed, the estimated NPV becomes important as a measure against which actual results are compared.

OTHER MEASURES

Although estimated NPV remains the most important measure in the Inception phase, other subjective and objective measures must be considered for those projects that will be funded.

Subjective measures such as

- **Customer satisfaction.** Is the sponsoring organization happy with progress being made?
- **Morale.** Is the project team happy with progress being made? Are they confident (at least guardedly so) about the likelihood for success?

Objective measures such as

- **Absolute progress.** As measured by whether the phase completed within expected time frames and completed the expected amount of work.

- **Requirements stability.** As measured by how much the project's goals changed over the course of the phase. A lot of change means that the project's goals may still be in flux, which would mean that the NPV estimates may be partially or fully suspect.
- **Risk stability.** As measured by how much the project's risks are still being discovered. It's hard to know what you don't know, so this is also partially a subjective measure, but if new major risks are still being discovered at a significant rate, it is a sign that you may not have a good enough understanding of the solution or the business needs to proceed.

Over the course of the project, you need to be gathering data and comparing it to expectations to keep the project on track. You will not have a lot of data on the following measures in the Inception phase, but you need to have mechanisms in place to gather the data before you leave the phase. In all these measures, trends are more important than absolute values.

- **Effort expended.** Actual versus expected
- **Defect discovery and fix trends.** Actual and expected
- **Risk discovery and mitigation.** Actual and expected
- **Unplanned work identified and implemented.** Including scope changes
- **Planned work implemented and tested.** Actual and expected

In all of these, the estimates are fairly coarse. For things like planned work, a map of scenarios onto iterations is sufficient. How to work with these measures in the subsequent phases of the project will be addressed in later chapters.

Taken together, these initial measures, coarse as they are, provide a framework for measuring project progress and health that will be used throughout the project to determine whether the project is on track.

It is worth noting that determining not to fund a project is a perfectly acceptable outcome of the Inception phase. This outcome should not be regarded as a failure, as long as the decision is based on measures of the business value to be delivered and the technical feasibility. In fact, deciding not to further fund the project may be the best possible outcome if it frees resources for other more worthy projects.

SUMMARY

Funding for projects depends on the outcome of the Inception phase, which must be measured in terms of the benefits and costs of the project—only then can a firm decision be made about whether to proceed. If stakeholders cannot agree that the time and cost estimates are credible, it is best to forego the project and turn your attention to more worthy efforts.

At this phase of the project, rough estimates of the business benefit—usually expressed in terms of *net present value* (NPV)— should be sufficient to establish that there is clear value in pursuing the project. As the NPV formula suggests, benefits received sooner are much more valuable than benefits received in the future. Benefits for projects driven by compliance regulations can be estimated in terms of penalty avoidance.

Estimating costs is possible by building some small but representative part of the system in order to extrapolate project cost and schedule data. It helps to choose a few representative scenarios and develop the software to deliver them. This early prototyping effort should help establish both of the following:

- Whether the project is technically feasible
- A quantitative measure of project schedule and cost

Mapping risks and making some educated guesses about the work needed to address them will give you a sense of what resources will be required, by iteration.

The Inception phase is usually allowed a single iteration, but it sometimes takes more than one to determine the business viability of the project due to unexpected difficulty in determining the project's technical or financial viability. Although the Inception phase can serve to produce something akin to an old-school feasibility study, it is typically essential to do some prototyping to explore the technical feasibility of the project.

There are two steps in determining financial viability:

1. Determining that the time to market factor is reasonable.
2. Calculating the net present value of the proposed solution.

If either the time to market or the ensuing NPV calculations are negative, the project is not worth pursuing. If the NPV is positive, the project may be worth pursuing, provided that it does not compete for funding with other higher-valued projects.

The most valuable question to ask about an estimate is not "Is it accurate?" but "How wide a range of values is possible?" It is best to analyze a number of scenarios to determine the expected-case and the worst-case values for NPV. Often, the decision to go ahead with a project is based on whether the worst-case NPV is within acceptable limits.

A sound basis for funding projects requires other measures to be considered. These include subjective measures, such as customer satisfaction and project team morale. More objective measures include absolute progress, requirements stability, and risk stability. In all these measures, trends are more important than absolute values.

Remember: A decision to *not* to fund a project is a perfectly acceptable outcome of the Inception phase, as long as the decision is based on measures of the business value to be delivered and the technical feasibility. Deciding not to further fund the project may be the best possible outcome if it frees resources for other more worthy projects.

11

. . .

WHAT TO MEASURE IN THE ELABORATION AND CONSTRUCTION PHASES

The Elaboration and Construction phases have a number of similarities that lead to comparable approaches to measurement: In both phases, the primary focus is producing executable releases that progressively implement an increasing amount of the desired functionality of the system. The primary differences between the two phases stem from the kinds of risks the phases address. The Elaboration phase deals with technical risks that affect the architecture of the solution, whereas the Construction phase deals with risks related to getting the bulk of the project work done on time and within budget. These differences lead to a slightly different focus in measurement during the different phases.

MEASUREMENT IN THE ELABORATION PHASE

The main focus of the Elaboration phase is to prove the basic technical approach used as the basis for estimates in the Inception phase, and to fill in the technical details necessary to ensure delivery of the solution in the future. If the technical risks are low, as in projects that add relatively minor functional enhancements to existing systems, based on a stable and proven architecture, the Elaboration phase is largely superfluous and constrained to testing the assertion that the proposed changes will not break the existing architecture. It is for this reason that certain *agile* approaches, such as Scrum and Extreme Programming (XP), lack an equivalent phase—they implicitly or explicitly assume that the architectural risks are low, and that any changes that may occur will emerge during normal development work later on.

The typical development work performed in the Elaboration phase is to implement any additional scenarios necessary to assure that the technical approach is sound and the rough schedule and cost data from the Inception phase are still reasonable. From a *planning* perspective, the main difference between the Elaboration and Construction phases is the choice of scenarios developed. In the Elaboration phase, the choice is driven by risk, with scenarios chosen because they will cause risks to be confronted.

Solving these technically challenging problems will increase the certainty that the chosen solution is technically sound, or more likely, it will resolve problems in the solution that, if left unresolved, could threaten the project. In working off the technical risks, valuable experience and information will be obtained, resulting in estimates and plans for the remainder of the project that will have much greater reliability. This will become an important factor when we consider measurement in the Construction phase.

From a staffing perspective, the main differences between the Elaboration and Construction phases are that the Elaboration phase tends to have an *exploratory* aspect and tends to be staffed with a smaller team focused on exploring the technical risks in the solution. This means that project costs tend not to scale up until the Construction phase, when the project team may be expanded to complete the remaining work.

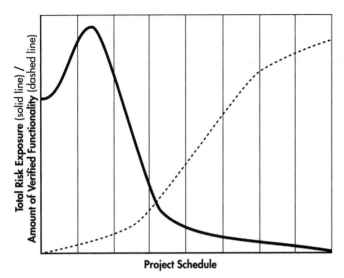

FIGURE 11.1 Expected risk and progress profiles for an iterative project

As noted previously, technical risk reduction is the main objective of the Elaboration phase. As a result, measurements in the phase focus on assessing whether technical risks are really declining. Figure 11.1 shows the typical risk profile for an effectively managed project (solid line) along with expected progress (dashed line). Iteration boundaries are marked by the vertical lines in the figure.

Notice that the total risks actually rise for an iteration or two early in the project. What causes the risks to start declining is the explicit confrontation of technical risks. The rapid drop in risks in the second and third iteration in the figure are due to the explicit focus on technical risks. The inflection point in the curve, the point at which the slope of the curve levels out, corresponds to the end of the Elaboration phase and the beginning of the Construction phase where technical risks have been mostly removed.

It is also important to measure progress starting early in the project. Figure 11.2 shows the expected profile of expected progress across the project lifecycle.

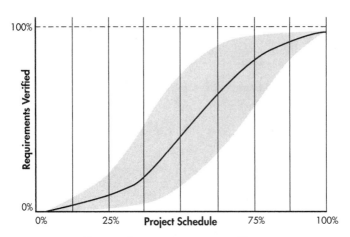

FIGURE 11.2 Expected project progress profile

In Figure 11.2, the gray area represents the normal expected range of possible progress observations, whereas the curved line represents an ideal progress profile. Notice that there is some progress even in the Inception phase (the initial one or two iterations), although progress remains slow as there may be a significant amount of rework as different technical approaches are tested and refined.

MEASURING RISK REDUCTION

It is a common practice for projects to develop a risk list early in the project, though fewer maintain this list over the course of the project. To ensure focus on the most important risks, this list can be abbreviated to the top 10 risks when reviewing it with others beyond the project team. An example is presented in Table 11.1.

The top 10 risks are selected based on their impact (rated from 1–10, with 1 being low impact and 10 being high impact) times their severity (rated from 1–10, with 1 being low severity and 10 being high severity). This number, the *risk rating*, is used to rank the risks,

TABLE 11.1 Example Top 10 Risks

Rank	Risk	Mitigation Results
1	Supporting previous ATM releases	Some progress made but not all issues resolved; keep at #1
2	Key staff member (Keith) departure	Cross-training complete; remove
3	Testing strategy, resources	Risk acceptably mitigated; remove
4	Estimates may be too optimistic	Risk seems within acceptable bounds, but keep on list
5	Scalability of the J2EE infrastructure	Some progress made, but not completely resolved; raise rank in next iteration
6	Reliability of O/S platform	Some progress made, but not completely resolved; raise rank in next iteration
7	Requirements not fully understood	Risk acceptably mitigated; remove
8	Fault tolerance	Some progress made; keep on list but lower rank
9	Tamper-proofing	Risk acceptably mitigated; remove
10	Printing flexibility and reliability	No progress made; raise rank in next iteration

and to measure the decrease in overall project risk. The expected risk profile (presenting the sum of the risk ratings for all risks over time) for an effectively managed project was shown in Figure 11.1.

If the overall risks are not declining from iteration to iteration, something is wrong—most often, the strategies the team is using to reduce risk are not being effective and risks continue unmitigated from iteration to iteration, or new risks are being found faster than old risks are being retired. In either case, a change in approach is needed. Perhaps the team lacks the technical experience to mitigate the technical risks, or perhaps the business environment is changing more rapidly than the project can respond. Whatever the case, failure to mitigate risks over a series of iterations is a sign that significant change in approach is required.

MEASURING PROGRESS

Progress can be measured by the number of scenarios that have been implemented and successfully tested. It is best to keep the measurement simple, ignoring for all practical purposes the fact that some scenarios are more complex than others. As shown in Figure 11.2, the progress curve rises slowly at first, as technical issues are resolved and the team gains experience working with one another. As the project enters the Construction phase, however, the project should have a fair amount of momentum and the iterations should be highly productive. Then, as the project nears its end, the rate of progress falls off as the finishing touches are put on the project.

The profile shown in Figure 11.2 can be obtained via a cumulative count of scenarios implemented and successfully tested. However, real-world progress is rarely a smooth upward progression. It more typically looks like Figure 11.3.

There is some rework to be expected when using an iterative approach as new ideas are tried and sometimes rejected, and as better solutions are devised when more information is available. The curve shown in Figure 11.2 shows the overall march of progress, but closer inspection of actual results would show something more like Figure 11.3—overall progress, with some setbacks.

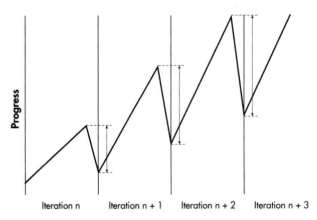

Iteration n   Iteration n + 1   Iteration n + 2   Iteration n + 3

FIGURE 11.3 The impact of rework on progress

Figure 11.3 actually shows an extreme case, with rework grow-ing over time, indicating some potential problems with the initial approach taken, and potentially the skills of the team. As a result, it is important to measure both overall progress as well as rework so as to have a better picture for what is really going on. Figure 11.4 shows expected rework trends over the lifecycle of the project.

Notice that rework is fairly significant early on, but declines significantly after the architecture is established at the end of the Elaboration phase.

Rework generally derives from defect identification, and defects should be captured from the start of the project. The typical trends for defects are shown in Figure 11.5. This figure shows that early in the project the software is relatively unstable, but by the end of the Elaboration phase the architectural instability has been brought under control.

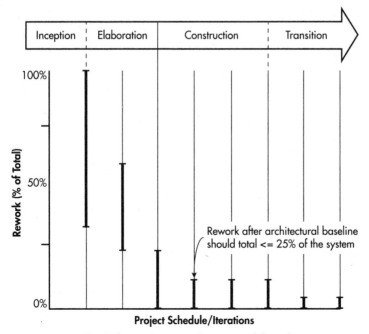

FIGURE 11.4 Rework trends across the project lifecycle

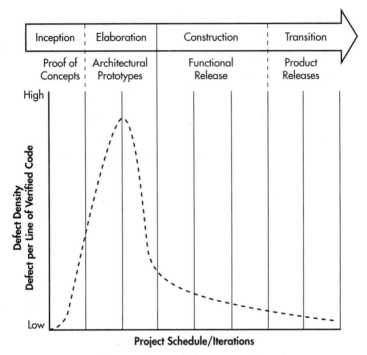

FIGURE 11.5 Defect trends across the project lifecycle

MEASUREMENT IN THE CONSTRUCTION PHASE

The main focus of the Construction phase is building the solution that was sketched in the Inception phase and "architected" in the Elaboration phase. You will identify any remaining requirements and develop and test the solution. By the end of the phase, you should have an operational system, though some rough edges may remain to smooth out.

In addition to the measurement performed in the Elaboration phase, a few new measurements are added:

- Backlog growth or shrinkage
- Test coverage
- Build stability

MEASURING THE PROJECT BACKLOG

The backlog consists of anything that you are not currently working on. The backlog grows as new things that need to be done are identified, and it shrinks as those things are implemented and tested. If it is still growing significantly by the time the Construction phase rolls around, something is wrong. By the end of the Construction phase, all scenarios must be implemented and tested, which means that the backlog must be declining throughout the phase and must reach zero (or close enough) by the end of the phase.

The backlog can be managed by declaring some items in it will be done in a future release, meaning that they are moved out of the current project's backlog and into the backlog for the future release. This often requires a fair amount of negotiation among stakeholders, but it is usually essential to managing the backlog.

MEASURING TEST COVERAGE

Implicit in the prior discussion about measuring progress was the notion that work is only counted as completed when it has been successfully tested. The recommended measure of progress is the completed scenario. Sometimes, largely because of staffing problems, it is difficult to thoroughly test all completed work. When this happens, two things are visible in the measurements: Progress will fall below expectations because there is a kind of "testing backlog," and test coverage will not grow as quickly as it should.

Some project teams make the mistake of counting the scenario as completed when the developers working on it have completed their work. Doing so is a mistake for two reasons:

1. It inflates the project progress, counting as completed things that may in fact be rejected for rework due to testing.
2. It masks the fact that the project may not be adequately staffed to complete the testing effort.

You need to test as you go along; testing is the only way you really know whether you are done with something. Testing always uncovers things that need to get done, so if you do not keep up with the testing effort you are falling behind. As you evaluate test results, you need to also keep an eye on the quality of the work being performed. Tests that fail are an indication that your progress may not be as good as you think it is.

To ensure that progress measures are not inflated, keep track of the test coverage—it should be at 100% for all completed scenarios. If a coverage gap is forming, you need to make immediate and deliberate efforts to reduce it to zero as soon as possible.

MEASURING BUILD STABILITY

A build is the result of the process whereby the code for the solution is compiled and linked into an executable version of the system. Effective build processes test the build by running automated tests against it to validate that it is working correctly. The results of the build and automated test process produce useful measures of project health.

Figure 11.6 shows the results of the build process over a sequence of days. Figure 11.6 also shows that although the builds have been successful on many days, there are also a number of days when the build was completely broken, and toward the end of the period it appears that results were very unstable. This could indicate that changes were introduced that affected many team members, and that the changes were poorly communicated. This could be a sign of deeper problems and should be investigated.

Even if you're the sort of manager who tends to leave the technical details to others on your team, you need to keep an eye on the build results. If you are working iteratively, you should be building frequently; if you are really working iteratively, you should be able to build continuously. If the build is often broken, it is a sign that

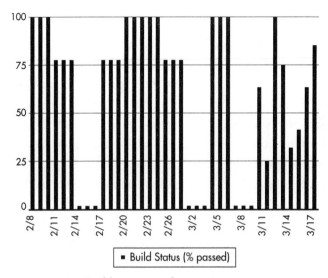

FIGURE 11.6 Build status trends over time

you are probably not as far along as you think you are, and you could be in real trouble from both a progress and quality perspective if the broken build is because of unresolved architectural issues.

EXPECTED PROGRESS TRENDS IN THE CONSTRUCTION PHASE

As previously noted, all planned work needs to be completed by the end of the Construction phase. The next and last phase of the project, the Transition phase, focuses on deploying the solution into a "production" environment; the Transition phase should not be turned into a "cleanup" phase in which the backlog continues to be worked down. There is enough work to do in deploying an application that continuing to implement scenarios is not an option.

One of the major questions to answer in the Construction phase is "Can we get all the necessary work done by the end of the phase?" Assessing the productivity of the team is important. You have to constantly look at the productivity of the team and assess the remaining backlog to determine if it can be reduced to zero. A useful, though subjective, measure is velocity, which can be approximated by the rate of change in the progress curve, or the rate of growth or shrinkage of the backlog. Based on whether the backlog is growing or shrinking, you can estimate the productivity of the team and make predictions about whether the backlog can be reduced to zero over the remainder of the phase. If it appears that it cannot, you have few alternatives: extend the length of the phase or negotiate the scope of the backlog downward.

SUMMARY

The primary purpose in both the Elaboration and Construction phases is producing executable releases that implement an increasing amount of the system's functionality. The differences in these phases have to do with the types of risks addressed: The Elaboration phase deals with technical risks affecting architecture, whereas the Construction phase deals with risks related to project scheduling and budget.

Elaboration Phase

The main focus of the Elaboration phase is to prove the basic technical approach used as the basis for estimates in the Inception phase, and to fill in the technical details necessary to ensure delivery of the solution in the future. Development work performed in the Elaboration phase produces any additional scenarios necessary to ensure a sound technical approach and that the rough schedule and cost data from the Inception phase are still reasonable. The choice of scenarios developed in Elaboration is driven by risk, with scenarios chosen because they will cause risks to be confronted. The Elaboration phase tends to be exploratory, staffed with a smaller team focused on exploring the technical risks in the solution. Measurements must focus on whether technical risks are declining.

Creating a risk list early in the project is a common practice, and abbreviating this to the top 10 risks ensures focus on the most important risks over the course of the project. The top 10 are selected based on the severity of impact. If the overall risks are not declining from iteration to iteration, a change in approach is needed. As risks decline, project progress can be measured by the number of scenarios that have been implemented and successfully tested.

There is some rework to be expected when using an iterative approach as new ideas are tried and sometimes rejected, and as better solutions are devised when more information is available. Rework may be fairly significant early on, but it usually declines significantly after the architecture is established at the end of the Elaboration phase.

Construction Phase

The main focus of the Construction phase is building the solution that was sketched in the Inception phase and "architected" in the Elaboration phase. The phase ends with an operational system, though some rough edges may remain. There are three new things to measure in this phase: backlog growth or shrinkage, test coverage, and build stability.

As you identify new things that need to be done, the backlog grows; as those things are implemented and tested, it shrinks. The backlog should not be growing significantly by the end of the Construction phase. If certain things remain in the backlog that are important to some stakeholders, but not critical to the first release of the system, these items can be moved out of the current project's backlog and into the backlog for a future release.

Sometimes it is difficult to thoroughly test all completed work. When this happens, progress falls below expectations because of a testing backlog, and test coverage will not grow as quickly as it should. Ideally, you test as you go along, bearing in mind that testing is the only way you really know whether something is finished. Testing always uncovers things that need to get done, so if you do not keep up with the testing effort, you are falling behind. Keep track of the test coverage, which should be at 100% for all completed scenarios.

Testing the build—a compiled and executable version of the system—requires you to run automated tests to validate that it is working correctly. The results of the build and automated test process produce useful measures of project health. You cannot afford to be a "hands-off" manager when it comes to build results. Iterative project teams should be building frequently; if you are really working iteratively you should be able to build continuously. If the build is often broken, you are probably not as far along as you think you are. In the worst cases, frequently broken builds are the result of unresolved architectural issues that were not properly addressed in the Inception or Elaboration phases.

The next and last phase of the project, the Transition phase, focuses on deploying the solution into a "production" environment.

12
• • •

WHAT TO MEASURE IN THE
TRANSITION PHASE

With the bulk of the development work behind, the goal of the Transition phase is to deploy the solution to its intended user base, which begins by deploying the developed solution into a production environment.

Measurement in the Transition phase is focused on assessing release readiness and wrapping up the project as a whole. This involves a range of different kinds of work:

- Final verification of all functionality.
- Defect fixing to resolve any issues that need to be handled prior to deployment.
- Installation and configuration of the final product in the production environment, including any data migration that may be needed. For many systems, data conversion and finally putting the application into production are complex problems that require significant attention; in some cases, the issues may be complex enough to warrant a separate project to just handle the deployment issues. In these cases, the development project deploys its solution to a staged

deployment environment, which is managed by the deployment project. In shops that support 24×7 customer access, a parallel "conversion" environment is often established. When the application is ready to be made generally available, users are migrated to it.

- Training of users. Few systems are so intuitively easy-to-use that their users do not require some training. Systems accessed directly by customers must provide some way to lead customers through a tutorial the first time they access the new system. Training may also include an introduction to changes to business processes being implemented in concert with the new system.

- Training of support staff. Just like machinery, systems must be maintained. During the Transition phase, the project might need to integrate the rollout and patching of the new system with the ongoing maintenance of the old system.

It's important to note that by the Transition phase, you absolutely should not be implementing new features or scenarios. If you are, you have simply fooled yourself into believing that you have exited the Construction phase. In the Transition phase, the sole focus should be getting the solution ready to deploy and then actually deploying it.

The Transition phase concludes when the solution has been successfully deployed and the maintenance and support responsibilities have been handed over to the team that will support and maintain the solution on an ongoing basis.

MEASUREMENT IN THE TRANSITION PHASE

The measurements to be made in the Transition phase focus on suitability of the system for deployment. This means focusing on test coverage and defect levels, including the relationship between defect discovery and defect close rates. The kinds of things you need to consider in order to determine suitability for deployment include:

- **Suitability for deployment.** Quality measures, including performance, scalability, and supportability measures in addition to traditional defect measures.
- **Adoption measures.** Especially measures related to the number of people actually using the solution, with an eye to answering the question "Are enough people using the release candidate to know whether it is meeting quality goals?"
- **User satisfaction.** This is usually as measured by reported defects, with indications as to whether the reporter of the defect considers the defect to be a "stop ship" defect (in other words, the defect reporter feels very strongly that the defect needs to be fixed before the solution is ready to deploy).

What to Measure

In order to gather information to assess release readiness, you need to test. Of course, testing of all types should have been ongoing throughout the project. The difference now is that your focus shifts to testing whether the various qualities of the system are within acceptable thresholds for release. Testing during the Transition phase provides raw data whose analysis will tell you whether you are ready to release. You need to test, at minimum:

- All "must have" requirements
- All requirements related to performance and scalability thresholds
- All requirements related to usability thresholds
- All requirements related to supportability—things that affect the way that the system will be serviced and supported after it is released

In other words, anything that would affect the releasability of the system needs to be tested, and the underlying requirements need to specify acceptable ranges for the measures. All "must have" requirements (requirements that must be satisfied by the system in order for it to be minimally acceptable) need to have acceptable ranges defined, and it is a good idea to define acceptable ranges for all "should have" requirements (requirements that should be satisfied by the system, but if not, the system would still meet minimal acceptability criteria) as well. If there are minimum performance or scalability goals that must be met, they need to be specified.

When testing scenarios, capturing measures on a pass/fail basis is usually sufficient. But for requirements related to performance and scalability, actual values are needed. Since trends are usually important, you need to gather a range of data observations. For example:

- The number of concurrent users the system can support, showing how response times vary as users are added. You need to simulate the transaction mix of the overall user community to provide an accurate picture, and the transactions need to be randomized to ensure that testing practices themselves do not bias the results.
- The data scalability of the system, showing how response times vary under an average transaction and user mix, but with varying amounts of data in storage. Many systems are sensitive not only to transaction workload but also data volumes.
- In real-time systems, the speed and capacity of data feeds and event timing is similarly important to measure.

Analyzing Trends and Assessing Test Results

It is a good idea to establish measurement goals for requirements, as in cases where minimum performance requirements are specified.

In almost all cases where a measurement goal is established, there will be ranges of acceptability, with minimal thresholds for the requirement to be met, along with test cases as proof of meeting each requirement. When these test cases are executed, the test results need to be analyzed to ensure that all actual results are within the acceptable range of values. Values falling outside acceptable ranges or failing to meet minimum acceptance criteria should result in defects that must be resolved before the solution can be deployed.

Trends for test data should be analyzed to assess whether the values, while currently within acceptable thresholds, might eventually stray outside. Sample data sets and user loads should be increased to the point where measurement thresholds are exceeded to see how much growth in system workload can be accommodated before performance or response times become unacceptable.

Tests producing results not within acceptable tolerances should result in defects being filed, enabling the resulting work to be tracked to completion.

Other Considerations Affecting Releasability

Harder to quantify but still essential is measuring the supportability of the system. This is usually done via a qualitative assessment of the discussions you have with the support staff for the solution. Support staff includes the people who will maintain the system as well as IT operations staff who will have to keep the system running.

Things you need to evaluate include:

- What is the status of hand-over activities? Has a "test deployment" (including data conversion if applicable) been performed? Was it successful? What issues were uncovered?
- What has the user adoption experience been? Is there sufficient confidence that the users will accept the new system?
- Is the support staff ready to take over support for the system? Do they have the necessary skills to support the solution?

Have procedures for backup and recovery, including disaster recovery, been updated and tested to ensure that they are effective?

• If the solution needs to be deployed to more than one system, is it sufficiently simple to ensure verifiable repeatability?

There is a tendency to overlook these factors when considering issues of releasability. Problems in these areas require technical resolution much earlier in the project, and the underlying needs should have been captured as requirements. The focus here is to ensure that the issues previously identified have been satisfactorily resolved.

CONCLUDING THE TRANSITION PHASE

The conclusion of the Transition phase is also the conclusion of the project. An evolution of the solution is complete, and a solution has been deployed to its users; the solution has been handed over to production support or the next project. Once the dust settles, it is a good time to step back and consider what went well, what could have gone better, and what went poorly. This is usually conducted as an open discussion among the participants on the project, led by an independent facilitator. The goal of the session is not to assign blame but to identify areas of improvement for future projects. In conducting the retrospective you should encourage people to reflect on the processes followed, identifying what worked well and any things that need improvement. Be as balanced as possible. For example:

• Focus on both good and bad.
• Be open and honest about what worked and what did not.
• Be nonjudgmental; separate "what was done" from "who did what."

We all need to learn from mistakes as well as successes, so don't sweep mistakes under the rug—being open and honest about what is working and what is not is important if you are to improve project success over time. Don't focus on assigning blame, but on what needs to be done to make the next project better. You should strive to create a learning culture in which experimentation for improvement is rewarded.

In preparation for the next evolution or project, you should develop recommendations about what to change next time; make decisions and put them into action. Learn from experience and communicate this knowledge to others so that other project teams can benefit from your experiences. Too often, we (the authors) have observed that iteration, phase, and project reviews result in little long-term change in behavior from project to project in the same organization. It is too easy to ascribe project problems to individuals or unique events. However, we know from experience that most problems are systemic and will repeat until the root causes are dealt with.

This is especially important when projects are part of a larger program. Generally, all projects in a program follow the same (or very similar) processes, and if the project problems are due to problems related to the process or related measurements used to monitor progress and risk, it is important to resolve these as early as possible so as not to have other projects in the program repeat the same problems. Program-based projects are the subject of the next chapter.

SUMMARY

Measurement in the Transition phase is focused on assessing release readiness, and on wrapping up the project as a whole. The goal is getting the solution ready to deploy and then actually deploying it. By the Transition phase, you should not be implementing new features or scenarios. If you are, you haven't exited the Construction phase. Types of measurements include suitability for deployment (quality measures and traditional defect measures); adoption measures (answer the question "Are enough people using the release candidate to know whether it is meeting quality goals?") and user satisfaction (number of reported defects and their severity).

Testing of all types should have been ongoing throughout the project, but in the Transition phase, you begin testing whether the various qualities of the system are within acceptable thresholds for release. You must, at minimum, test all "must have" requirements; all requirements related to performance and scalability thresholds; all requirements related to usability thresholds; all requirements related to supportability—things that affect the way the system will be serviced and supported after it is released.

Usually establishing a measurement goal means establishing ranges of acceptability, with minimal thresholds for the requirement to be met, along with test cases as proof of meeting each requirement. Results of these tests need to be analyzed, and values falling outside acceptable ranges point to defects that need to be resolved before the solution can be deployed.

System "supportability" is harder to quantify, and is usually done via a qualitative assessment of the discussions you have with the support staff for the solution. You need to evaluate the status of transition activities, such as a "test deployment" and any issues found; confidence that the users will accept the new system; readiness of the support staff; and if multiple systems are involved in deploying the solution, is it sufficiently simple to ensure verifiable repeatability?

When the Transition phase is complete, the project is complete, and it's time for conducting a retrospective. Encourage people to reflect on the processes followed, identifying what worked well and any things that need improvement. Be as balanced as possible. We all need to learn from mistakes as well as successes, so don't sweep mistakes under the rug—it is important to be open and honest about what is working and what is not if you are to improve project success over time. Develop recommendations about what to change next time; make decisions and put them into action. Learn from experience and communicate this knowledge to others so that other project teams can benefit from your experiences.

13

. . .

MEASURING PROJECTS EMBEDDED IN PROGRAMS

Now that we've covered the ways to measure project health during the essential phases of an iterative software development project, let's consider a larger context for the single project we've been describing. Frequently, we must manage projects embedded in a larger program, which requires assessing project health and value delivery from a cross-project perspective. Projects that comprise a program are inextricably linked, and problems in one project can threaten the health of the overall program success. Spotting problems early enables you to address them earlier, potentially saving the program.

A program is a group of related projects managed in a coordinated way. Programs usually include an element of ongoing work. Here are a few examples:

- Strategic programs, in which projects share vision and objectives
- Business cycle programs, in which projects share budget or resources but might differ in their vision and objectives

- Infrastructure programs, in which projects define and deploy supporting technology used by many other projects, resulting in shared standards
- Research and development programs, in which projects share assessment criteria
- Partnership programs, in which projects span collaborating organizations

There are often variations on these programs that combine different aspects from several types. The important thing to remember is that a program organizes projects to focus attention on the delivery of a specific set of strategic business results. True programs differ from large projects in that they focus on the delivery of a step change in an organization's capability, which in turn can affect all aspects of the business, including the business processes, financial structures, and information technology.

Examples of different kinds of projects that can benefit from coordination within a program include:

- The development project that builds the software
- A project to train the users of the system
- A project to upgrade servers and infrastructure for the new system
- A project to train the support personnel

Because the type of work performed on each of these is quite different, it makes sense to have a separate project for each; but because all the projects need to be successful for the business value to be delivered, a program is needed to manage the overall effort.

ORGANIZING PROJECTS INTO PROGRAMS

Organizing projects into programs provides explicit oversight for, and coordination between, the individual projects. Sometimes, additional management is needed so that the benefits achieved by

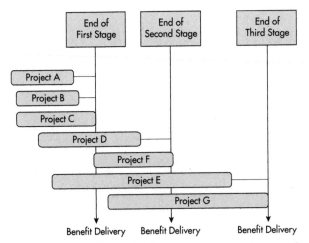

FIGURE 13.1 Relationship between program stages and projects

executing the projects in a coordinated way is greater than that which would accrue if the projects were all executed individually. Within a program, projects often share objectives and have a common process, at least to the degree that they will share milestones, measurements, and review criteria.

To distinguish between project iteration milestones and phase-ends, we will introduce the concept of a "stage." In effect, a stage is to a program what an evolution is to a project—it is used to manage a concerted effort toward some common end. The relationship between program stages and projects is shown in Figure 13.1.

Each stage delivers an incremental change in organizational capability. The end of a stage provides a major review point at which the program results can be evaluated and assessed against desired outcomes.

Stages can be used to group related projects, as shown in Figure 13.2.

Just like the evolutions of a software development project, the stages can overlap, building upon one another and sharing objectives as they incrementally deliver products as part of a

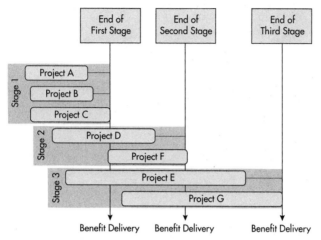

FIGURE 13.2 Using program stages to group projects with shared goals

larger, coordinated program. Because most programs are long lived (some last for decades), there many be an unlimited number of stages in a program.

Figure 13.3 shows how work can be organized within a stage, with the stage governed by a control project. Notice how the phases for the control project sometimes end a little later than the corresponding phases of the projects it manages. This enables the results from the managed projects to be rolled up to the control project.

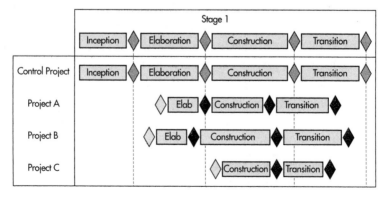

FIGURE 13.3 Using control projects to govern program stages

How is a stage managed in practice? The control project starts the stage by discovering the overall stage goals and desired outcomes for the stage as a whole, and by creating or updating the overall architecture to be shared by all projects within the stage. As the architecture stabilizes, additional projects in the stage are initiated and overseen by the control project. Each stage would have its own control project for management purposes.

MEASURING PROGRAM STAGES

Because each stage is independent of other stages, each one can and should be managed separately. The control project provides a useful control and measurement vehicle for the stage, and the same measures for projects that were discussed in earlier chapters can be applied to a control project managing a program stage. The control project goes through the same lifecycle as a project evolution; it goes through all four phases—Inception, Elaboration, Construction, and Transition—in the Unified Process lifecycle.

The control project, however, is different from a normal project in that most of the real work of the stage occurs in the subprojects coordinated by the control project. Therefore, measurements of the control project need to consolidate and roll up the measurements from the subprojects within the stage. For example, the risks and issues from the subprojects would be consolidated to form the risks and issues for the control project. Other project health measurements can be rolled up in similar ways to form a view of how the stage is progressing.

SUMMARY

Frequently, we must manage projects embedded in a larger program—a group of related projects managed in a coordinated way. Managing projects embedded in a larger program requires assessing project health and value delivery from a cross-project perspective. Such projects are inextricably linked, so problems in one project can threaten the health of the overall program. Spotting and addressing problems early enables you to potentially save the program.

A program organizes projects around the delivery of a specific set of strategic business results. True programs differ from large projects: They focus on the delivery of a step change in an organization's capability, which in turn can affect all aspects of the business, including the business processes, financial structures, and information technology. When the type of work performed on a variety of projects is quite different, it makes sense to manage them as separate projects for each; but when all of these projects need to be successful in order for the business value to be delivered, then a program is needed to manage the overall effort.

Programs usually include an element of ongoing work—for example, strategic programs, in which projects share vision and objectives, and business cycle programs, in which projects share budget or resources but might differ in their vision and objectives.

Within a program, projects often share objectives and have a common process, at least to the degree that they will share milestones, measurements, and review criteria. The end of a phase in a program is called a stage, and it is used to manage concerted effort toward some common end. Each stage delivers an incremental change in organizational capability. The end of a stage provides a major review point at which the program results can be evaluated and assessed against desired outcomes.

Stages are managed separately, and are measured and controlled by a control project that consolidates and rolls up the measurements from the subprojects within the stage. The real work of the stage occurs in the subprojects coordinated by the control project.

APPENDIX

• • •

GETTING STARTED WITH ITERATIVE
PROJECT MANAGEMENT

"Desirable ends do not come of themselves. Men must conceive them, believe in them, further them, and execute them."
—Carl Van Doren

This book has presented an approach to improving business results through the systematic application of the principles of iterative development, but the principles do not apply themselves. In this appendix,[1] we present practical advice on adopting these practices within your organization. We realize that you come to the subject of iterative project management with different goals and different constraints on how much change you can introduce. You may be someone who is:

- Completely new to managing iterative development projects and about to start on your very first iterative project
- Already engaged in managing iterative projects and struggling to put the theory into practice

---

1. Excerpted from Kurt Bittner and Ian Spence, *Managing Iterative Software Development Projects* (Addison-Wesley, 2007).

- Already managing iterative development projects and looking to improve and validate your approach
- Engaged in rolling out or supporting the rollout of iterative development techniques to your department or organization

To support all these views and more, this chapter looks at how you can apply what you have learned to

- Implement your first project
- Build on your current success
- Help change your organization

We discuss how you can start to apply the techniques immediately to the projects that you manage and how you can build upon this success to progressively expand your use of iterative software development practices.

EMBARKING ON YOUR FIRST ITERATIVE PROJECT

Embarking on your first iterative project probably fills you with some uneasiness, and you might have some doubts about your project taking on what you might perceive to be additional risk. In this section we help you take that first step.

Why Iterate?

As we have noted a number of times in the course of this book, iterative development is undertaken to eliminate project risks early in the project, before they can have a chance to sink the project. By tackling risk explicitly, your project will be more likely to succeed. That alone should provide fairly powerful motivation. Other reasons for adopting an iterative approach include

- To achieve higher quality
- To achieve faster results

- To achieve results more reliably, or sometimes just to achieve results at all
- To reduce staff frustration and turnover
- To achieve greater flexibility and business agility
- To reduce costs

Understanding these and any other goals is important so that you can factor them into the actions that you and your team will take.

The impetus for change can come from any number of sources: from senior management wanting to achieve better business results, from senior technical leaders wanting to resolve recurrent project problems, or from project teams that want to improve themselves. Whatever the source, the stimulus for change tends to gestate until a sponsor picks it up.

There also needs to be a sense of urgency about the need to change; some crisis or significant opportunity is required to get the project team members to be interested in the extra work of learning how to do something new. Change is initiated for a variety of reasons. The reasons listed here are the major themes that lie behind most change initiatives. Often the reasons for the change are not well articulated or even well understood.

Unless there is a sense of urgency, the stimulus for change will never become great enough to overcome resistance. People become comfortable with the status quo, and it is difficult to get them to change unless they feel that they will personally benefit from the change. They need to believe that unless they change the way they work, bad things will happen, or in the case of opportunities, good things will fail to happen.

This is not to say that threatening or frightening people is an effective motivational technique. (It is not.) It merely observes that people need to feel that if they don't change, they will fail. In the early stages of a change, only a few people might feel this need to change. As long as the change is small enough that it only affects a small group, this is sufficient to move ahead.

Potential Barriers to the Adoption of Iterative Practices

Before you start, you need to understand the potential barriers to the change so that you can make the right choices of timing, project, and approach. Some of the more important questions to ask include the following:

- *How supportive is senior management of the change?* The measurements and milestones they establish can easily derail an iterative approach, as is the case when they ask even seemingly innocent questions such as "When will the design be completed?" or "When will requirements be signed-off?"

- *What is the scope of your authority to make changes?* How much of the development lifecycle are you responsible for? For example, the requirements might have already been specified in a format and to a level of detail that would make it more difficult to adopt an iterative approach.

- *What are the team's feelings about the changes?* How enthusiastic is the team about iterating? To achieve the transition to iterative development, you will need the support of the team, especially the other members of the leadership team.

- *What else does the team have to do?* How many other projects and initiatives is the team involved in? If the team is not focused on and dedicated to the project, the transition to iterative practices will probably be slower and take more time and energy to complete.

- *What capability do you need to improve?* It is important to understand the capability of the team and how well the current capability supports the proposed iterative approach. For example, is there any testing capability in the team? Testing will be needed from the first iteration, which is often a problem in companies organized around the phases of a waterfall process where the expectation is that testers will only be needed late in the project lifecycle.

- *What work has already been done?* No project starts from nothing. You need to know what products and artifacts have already been produced.
- *Where are you in the project lifecycle?* It is important to understand the state of the project. Changes are easier to make during an evolution's Inception and Elaboration phases than they are during its Construction and Transition phases.[2]

Selecting the right project and the right team members for the initial effort is important. Table A.1 presents some of the key characteristics to look for in your first iterative project.

The lack of these characteristics does not, by itself, present an insurmountable problem, but it will slow the pace of the project, in particular extending the first two phases where the major business and technical risks are addressed.

When you start your first iterative project, factor the successful adoption of iterative techniques into the critical success factors for the project and the career development objectives for the team members. This is especially important if circumstances require an investment in training and mentoring the team to enable the transformation to take place.

Conventional wisdom suggests that you should choose low-impact, non critical projects to be the focus of early change efforts to reduce the change effort's risk and the potential for failure. The problem with this is that although these projects are lower risk, their non criticality usually means that they are starved for resources and not considered "mainstream" enough to ever be taken seriously as success stories. This dooms the overall change initiative. Low-priority projects are not visible enough to engender the support needed to drive the change forward.

---

2. You can still evaluate a project using the Unified Process lifecycle even if the project is not being run using the Unified Process and even if it is not being run iteratively. The questions in the phase checklists can be applied to any project, and the answers will provide valuable insight into the project's state and outstanding risks.

TABLE A.1 The Characteristics of a Good First Iterative Project

Characteristic	Description	Reason
Attitude	Iterative development needs a team that wants to iterate (or at least to try new approaches).	"Unbelievers" will revert to their old ways of working, masking this by using "iterative" terms.
Project Size	The project needs to big enough to have at least four iterations but small enough that it will deliver results in four to six months. You want to choose projects that can demonstrate rapid success in dealing with real problems.	It will take a few iterations for the benefits to be accepted by the team. The team will need time to get used to the new ways of working.
Team Composition	Iterative development requires a full development team to be in place.	The team might be small but needs to cover all the software development disciplines all the time. Testers are needed early and throughout the project, not just at the end.
Technical Leadership	You need the support of people who can accurately gauge technical risk and help you to use this assessment to drive the definition and mitigation of technical risks.	The selection of appropriate risk reduction strategies requires a high level of technical knowledge about the proposed solution. The management team relies on the architecture team to successfully guide the project through the Elaboration phase.
Business Criticality	The project needs to be business-critical enough to get the attention and involvement of stakeholders throughout the project.	Stakeholder involvement is needed throughout the project if the full benefits of iterative development are to be achieved.

Instead you should

- Look for a *small* number of must-do projects that have organizational focus and strong support
- Look for projects with a smaller set of stakeholders to keep communication simpler
- Look for projects with high internal visibility—ones that would make good success stories
- Choose projects that are short- to medium-term in length
- Staff the projects with the best people available (respected leaders)
- Organize projects to generate short-term wins—divide work into iterations
- Keep project size small in the first few iterations and then scale up
- Focus on choosing the right projects and committing resources to them

Choosing critical projects sounds risky, but there is no sense in hiding from the facts that only critical projects will get the attention and resources necessary to succeed. The key is choosing projects critical enough to get resources but that can start small and then scale up in a controlled way, not becoming too large before the architecture and technical risks can be brought under control. Scaling up should be targeted for the Construction phase but not before.

Communicating the Goals of Change

To motivate the change in approach, you must be able to clearly and concisely communicate why a different approach is needed. If the business goal is to achieve better responsiveness to changing market needs, the goal for the iterative project effort might be something like *be able to go from idea to released product in nine months* (*or less!*). The more precise and measurable the goals, the easier they are to achieve.

It's important for you to do a couple things when you are communicating the reasons for the change:

- **Be concise and articulate, and be able to explain it in a few minutes or less.** The vision needs to be precise and specific, without sounding like empty slogans exhorting people to "do better." It should set specific goals that can be translated into criteria by which people can make decisions.
- **Link problems to outcomes, such as "If we don't do X better, Y will happen."** Linking problems to outcomes is essential to getting a sense of urgency to solving the problem. Being specific is also important. Generalization is easy but not very compelling. Ultimately you need to set specific goals. Being specific about the problem and its impact sends this message from the beginning. For example, "Our inability to deliver releases within X% of the projected date results in lost opportunities of Y million dollars per year" directly links the problem to its outcome.

You must communicate this vision at every possible opportunity, at every level of the organization. Everyone should understand what is being done and why. Being able to concisely describe it in a few minutes comes from the idea of an "elevator pitch"—think of a chance meeting in an elevator with a key decision maker. You have this person's undivided attention for, at most, a few minutes. The vision needs to be crisp, concise, and compelling enough to explain in just these few minutes. Everyone today is busy; they don't have time to carefully read pages and pages of reasoning and justification. Set it out for them, and your message will have a better chance of being internalized. The vision need not be very specific about how the change will be achieved, but it does need to be compelling.

Kotter[3] observes that failure to communicate the vision is a key factor in failed change efforts. You will probably need to communicate the vision 10 to 100 times more often than you are probably planning to do. People usually focus on the impact and cost of changing; everyone needs to understand the impact of not changing. Only when people feel that their outcomes will suffer if they don't change will the change really take root.

Determining the Pace of Change

Every person and every project has a limited tolerance for change. People who have been successful with change initiatives in the past are more likely to embrace change, whereas people and projects that have a mixed or poor record of success with change will be more resistant to change. Trying to make too many changes too fast will be destabilizing and will make things worse, at least for a period of time. Most people have a threshold to the pace of change that they can sustain — try to push change faster, and the entire effort can stall and fall apart. The ability of the people to deal with change needs to be taken into account when planning change.

If the change is too large, people may lose hope that it will ever pay off and may abandon it. We have personally witnessed this many times, which is why we recommend an iterative approach to introducing change. This seems like simple common sense and no great innovation, but it remains a mystery to us why people so often try to push large changes in a single large initiative.

Expectations must be carefully managed. The tendency for teams to want to do everything immediately needs to be tempered; a sense of "proportion and pace" is crucial. The improvements must be driven fast enough to achieve the desired results as quickly as possible, but not so fast that the team gets confused or disheartened at lack of progress due to too much change at once.

---

3. John P. Kotter, *Leading Change* (Harvard Business School Press, 1996).

Dealing with Skepticism

You will encounter skepticism and disbelief in the approach that you are proposing. You should be prepared to answer the skeptics because they are likely to be your biggest supporters if you can win them over. Everyone has seen grand new approaches that claim wonderful benefits but fail to produce results. The skeptics will ask, "What will be different this time?" The argument is based on the observation that every project manager starts every project with a new plan and the best of intentions, but the result is always the same: project slips, frustration, and failure. You must be able to answer the question, "Why should we believe you are doing something significant enough to affect the outcome?"

We have encountered this question often enough to have some thoughts on how to answer it. Appropriate responses include the following:

- "We recognize that change is inevitable, and we are taking an approach that recognizes that. We will set goals for our progress, we will measure ourselves against those goals, and we will adapt our approach in light of new information rather than assuming that we had all the answers at the start of the project, which you know is not true."
- "We will focus on the big risks early, while we can still do something about them, and we will take explicit action to reduce those risks. If our first attempts do not work, we will keep at them until we have dealt with the risks."
- "We will focus on delivering the most important things the business *really needs* in an agreed-upon time frame rather than delivering everything they want. This is an important change from how we have done things in the past."

In short, you need to say and show how the iterative approach is pragmatic and deals with the realities of the real world. Although real convincing comes only with the proof provided by real progress, most skeptics find the honesty of statements like these to be refreshing, provided that they are backed up with actions.

Starting with Just Iterative Development

As discussed in Chapter 2, "What Is Iterative Development?" iterative behavior can be thought of as starting from the activity of developers. For a project to be considered iterative, it is essential that the software be developed iteratively—that is, the core development disciplines of Analysis, Design, and Implementation (which includes developer-driven testing) are applied repeatedly to evolve the software. Fortunately, this is the most natural way for developers to work. As Figure A.1 shows, when these disciplines are executed in an iterative fashion, additional disciplines can be added around the core development ones to get the whole team iterating in an effective and collaborative manner.

In some organizations, where waterfall development has become so entrenched that it has influenced the organizational structure and management responsibilities, you might find that

- The development work does not start until the requirements work is complete, and/or
- The other stakeholders and managers in the organization are very suspicious and don't believe that iterative development is suitable for them.

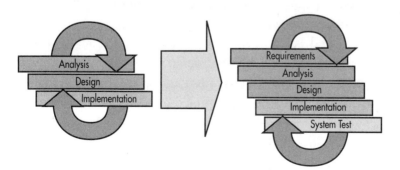

FIGURE A.1 Development (Analysis, Design, Implementation) lies at the core of the iterative approach

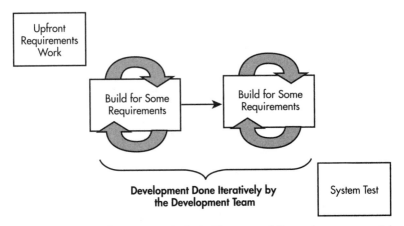

FIGURE A.2 Developing iteratively inside a waterfall requirements model

In this case, you can still apply and benefit from iterative development and project management techniques by adopting the "requirements pipeline" pattern shown in Figure A.2.

This compromise is often adopted in organizations new to iterative development, and it reflects the fact that the desire to iterate commonly originates in the development teams. To prove their iterative development capability, they will start to develop the software iteratively while the requirements and overall system testing are done in the traditional manner. In this case, the job of the development team is made easier if the requirements are captured in a form that enables the identification of sensible chunks of work to be implemented in the iterations.

After the development team has demonstrated the capability to implement sets of requirements in an iterative fashion, you can then expand the scope of the iterations to include the requirements and assessment disciplines. The projects will not be truly iterative in the way we have described throughout the rest of the book until you change the way that the development team works with the business.

Bootstrapping an Iterative Project

Starting your first iterative project is really just like starting any other iterative project. The approach follows these steps:

- Start with a small team focused on the business and technical risks.
- Challenge the team to start with a four-week iteration.
- Adjust the iteration length in response to work and team culture.
- Plan to deliver benefit every three to six months.
- Plan releases as well as iterations.
- Start with a colocated team.
- Address the architectural risks before scaling up.

Regardless of how large the project might appear to be, keep the following points in mind:

- **Start with the assumption that it is small.** If you start big, it will stay big, and generally the larger a project, the more likely it is to fail.
- **Do everything within your power to keep the project small.** If you don't fight to keep things small, they will naturally tend to get large.
- **Layer the plans and keep them succinct and focused.** To be comprehensible, plans must be small. Exploit the layering inherent in iterative projects to avoid unnecessary precision in planning the work.

The first iteration of your first iterative project will be the hardest to plan and manage; chances are you won't know exactly what to do and neither will your team, and this uncertainty is unsettling. It is also likely to be a new experience for the stakeholders as well as the project team, which will only compound the problems. To compensate for this, make sure that the iteration has modest objectives:

whatever you do, don't set yourself and the team up to fail by setting ridiculously aggressive objectives.

If you are following the advice presented in this book, then the iteration should be of average length (we recommend four weeks but are prepared to accept four to six weeks as a starting point). It is common for initial iterations to run over their schedule. Allowing this to happen establishes a bad precedent. Keep an eye on progress during the iteration and be ready to scale back on ambitions even in the middle of the iteration to make sure that you will have time to assess results. This usually means moving some scope from the current iteration to the next in order to maintain the iteration time box. When you assess the iteration, you can decide whether to make future iterations longer.

Your first iteration will probably be over planned. Don't worry; just keep learning and looking for ways to simplify the plans. The main trap to watch out for is overly aggressive planning, especially overestimating the productivity of a new team adopting new practices. If the team becomes demoralized, it will be impossible to get the project back on track, so set reasonable goals early and then ramp up expectations when the team is executing effectively.

Overly aggressive planning has other side effects on the expectations of external stakeholders. These stakeholders tend to focus almost exclusively on whether you did what you said you were going to do, and they will notice if you miss a milestone or if the project consistently fails to meet the commitments you have made to them and the other parts of the organization. The results of overly aggressive planning are illustrated by the following story.

> We once met a project manager who, having failed to complete the Elaboration phase in the predicted number of iterations, needed to adjust his plans. The reason that the phase could not be completed successfully was that the architectural baseline could not be tested because no hardware was available to run the tests.

On inquiring of the supplier when the hardware was likely to be available, the supplier responded that delivery would take at least six weeks, and that could only be achieved because they were such a valued customer and could be promoted to the top of the queue.

Learning this did not stop the project manager from re-planning the phase by adding one four-week iteration to the plan. The hardware predictably failed to magically appear earlier than promised, and the project again failed to complete the testing. This repeated failure to achieve the milestone led to a complete loss of trust between the project manager and the steering committee, and it also caused the manager's removal from the project.

It will take some time and effort to achieve the full benefits of an iterative approach. Your first evolution is unlikely to accomplish more than successfully producing the same amount of software in a non-iterative fashion, but there will be less rework, the project will be less risky, and the chances of delivering in the predicted time scales will be increased. As a result, it is important that you do not set unrealistic expectations for what can be achieved. Iterative development is not necessarily *faster* than traditional development, but you will be more certain of delivering the right result in an acceptable amount of time.

Keeping Going

The more you iterate, the better you and your team will get at it. Each iteration results in management, planning, process adoption, and team interactions improving and iteration becoming easier. By struggling through the first few iterations, you and the team learn how to iterate and how to work together in an iterative fashion. Over time, the levels of planning, reporting, designing, and everything else will settle at a natural level suitable for the team and the project. You achieve this by reviewing results at the end of each iteration and adapting your tactics and plans, discarding or amending things that don't add value and adding techniques as needed to resolve issues.

It will probably take you and your team a number of evolutions to become really proficient at iterating. The key is to keep going and use the evolutionary and iterative nature of the projects to evolve the team's capability alongside the solutions that they are developing. Achieving continuous improvement through iteration is the subject of the next section.

ADOPTING AN ITERATIVE APPROACH ITERATIVELY

One of the most powerful things about iterative development is that it provides a platform for continuous process improvement. The adaptive nature of the management and development processes means that you can do more with your project's agility than just respond reactively to change—you can also respond proactively to the lessons learned and the trends exhibited by the project to continuously improve the project's working practices and performance.

Understanding Where to Start

Although we hope that by this point in the book you accept that iterative development and iterative project management are useful tools to deliver better results, we recognize that you cannot get there all at once. Your initial iterative projects are unlikely to immediately exhibit all the desirable characteristics of an ideal iterative project. In our experience, it takes the typical project team at least three evolutions to start to exhibit all the desired behavior and establish themselves as experts in iterative development. *Iterative development* covers a broad set of behaviors and cultural values that emerge over time when teams are focused on results. In choosing an approach to phase in improvements, we have found the model

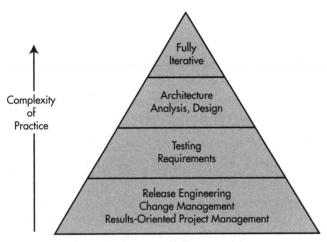

Complexity of Practice

Fully Iterative

Architecture Analysis, Design

Testing Requirements

Release Engineering
Change Management
Results-Oriented Project Management

FIGURE A.3 The foundations of software development

depicted in Figure A.3 useful when thinking about what improvements must come first.

As shown in Figure A.3, the foundation of iterative development is provided by a shift in project management focus away from creating detailed plans and measuring activities against these plans to results-oriented project management. As we have discussed in earlier chapters, software development is inherently creative and somewhat unpredictable. This means that the precisely appropriate approach is also not entirely predictable. Focusing attention on setting the right goals for each iteration and measuring achievements against those goals is the first and most important step in adopting iterative development.

Introducing effective practices in the areas of release engineering and change management (specifically basic versioning, baselining, and control over the things the project is producing) is essential to supporting this shift to becoming "results oriented." The ability to manage change across iterations (to determine which changes should be addressed in each iteration) and the ability to create executable releases (which requires a reliable build process) are essential to being able to make the shift to delivering objective results.

These basic skills can take you a long way, and in fact they provide most of what you need to perform maintenance and defect fixing across a series of iterations. This covers a great deal of software development activity, and most organizations would gain tremendous benefit if they only did these three things well.

If you are involved in new product development or are making larger and more significant evolutions to the software, you will need to add some additional skills, primarily the ability to understand needs and define requirements (referred to as "Requirements" in Figure A-3) and requirements-driven testing. If you need to build a completely new solution, you will probably not have the luxury of building upon an existing architecture. You will need to have a more disciplined way of forming the architecture of the system and translating requirements into designs.

As the solutions become more complex, you will need to draw upon all these skills in a fully iterative approach that is able to dynamically respond to new risks and find creative solutions to new problems.

The main reasons for presenting this model are first, to illustrate that most projects can get a lot of value from a basic focus on the fundamentals of results-oriented project management, release engineering, and change management without formalizing the approaches used for requirements, testing, architecture, analysis, or design, and second, to demonstrate that improvements in requirements management, testing, analysis, or architecture must be built on a good foundation of the "lower-order" techniques.

Improving Practices Iteratively

When applying this model to make improvements in a gradual or "progressive" manner, you should not strive to first become "perfect" at the lower levels before moving up to the next level. Instead, we recommend the approach depicted in Figures A.4 to A.6.

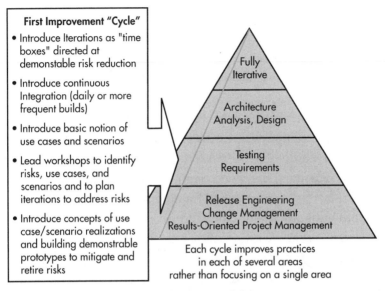

FIGURE A.4 Improvements in the first "cycle"

We recommend introducing new practices iteratively, in a sense taking a "slice" of a set of the overall practices that are to be introduced and implementing them in a series of iterations. We refer to this "slice" as an "improvement cycle," which could be a single iteration or could be as long as an evolution depending on the scope of the improvements being made. An improvement cycle consists of one or more iterations over which you will introduce some changes and then measure the results. The concept of an "improvement cycle" aligned with a specific set of iterations enables change to be introduced gradually and in a controlled way so that you can make sure that a more basic set of improvements has been successful before you introduce additional change.

As noted in Figure A.5, early improvement cycles introduce simple concepts such as the notion of an *iteration* as a time box in which specific results are achieved. The shift to a *results-oriented* perspective from an *activity-oriented* one is important, and it represents a big leap for many people, so you don't want to confuse people by introducing lots of other changes at the same time. We have found that the improvements listed in Figure A.4 tend to be the most important changes to introduce first.

The early improvement cycles are specifically *not* focused on formality or matters of style because this tends to derail success and gets people focused on formality and not results. The key point is to introduce some improvements from each "level" in a lightweight way and only to the degree that the changes improve results so as not to introduce too much change at once. Figures A.5 and A.6 show that as the team becomes comfortable with basic skills, the scope of the improvement effort can expand. Improvement cycles continue as long as the team feels that the improvements are adding value and reducing risk.

Specific improvements are driven by issues identified in iteration assessments to keep them focused on practical project needs. This approach enables the team to make progress and improve results while still getting useful work done. The boxes in the figures indicate the kinds of improvements that are *typical* in early and later improvement cycles.

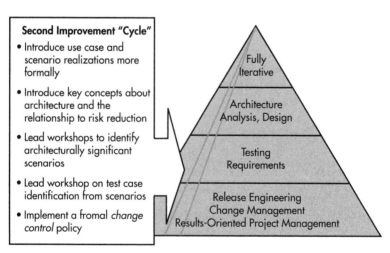

FIGURE A.5 Improvements in subsequent early "cycles"

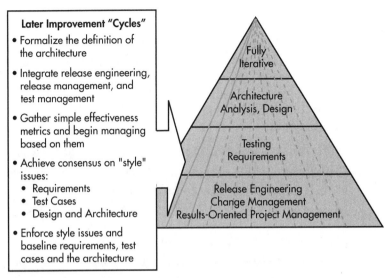

Later Improvement "Cycles"
- Formalize the definition of the architecture
- Integrate release engineering, release management, and test management
- Gather simple effectiveness metrics and begin managing based on them
- Achieve consensus on "style" issues:
  - Requirements
  - Test Cases
  - Design and Architecture
- Enforce style issues and baseline requirements, test cases and the architecture

Fully Iterative

Architecture Analysis, Design

Testing Requirements

Release Engineering
Change Management
Results-Oriented Project Management

FIGURE A.6 Improvements in later "cycles"

The essence of this approach is to introduce techniques in each improvement cycle to address the specific needs of the team rather than adopting a set of techniques wholesale. This enables the project team to show results *while* they are improving rather than letting the improvement effort stand in the way of producing results. This overcomes much of the traditional resistance to change.

Learning by Doing

The advantage of this approach is that people learn by doing, and they learn only what they immediately apply. The conventional wisdom (as practiced in much of the industry) is that change is introduced by defining the new processes, selecting supporting tools, and then training everyone on the new processes and tools. As it turns out, this approach actually increases the risk that the change will fail—the opposite of the intended result.

Training is necessary but on its own is not sufficient and is often over-emphasized at the expense of less formal experiential learning. To understand why, let's consider five stages of learning:[4]

1. **Knowledge**—Basic knowledge of the concepts and the facts
2. **Comprehension**—Demonstrated understanding of concepts
3. **Application**—Ability to apply concepts in simple contexts
4. **Evaluation**—Ability to apply judgment on when and how to apply concepts to more complex contexts
5. **Innovation**—Ability to extend concepts to new contexts

All that can be expected from a training class is to convey basic knowledge and *maybe* to provide some practice in applying the concepts. Time and experience are needed for the change to actually take hold in the day-to-day activities of the team. Only when this occurs is the change successful.

To achieve sustainable results, change must be driven by doing real work. There are several reasons for this:

- People don't like to change, but they will change if they can see that change leads to positive outcomes. "Positive outcomes" means different things to different people. For management, it might mean more reliable schedules and improved delivery capability. For the people on the project, it might mean improved career development or improved quality of life. Successful change initiatives usually require the majority of stakeholders to achieve some positive result. The sooner positive results are shown, the sooner support for the change builds.
- Even positive changes are initially disruptive; few situations are so bad that change is not initially destabilizing. In addition, most changes take some time to produce results.

---

4. These are loosely adapted from Benjamin S. Bloom's *Taxonomy of Educational Objectives* (Boston: Allyn and Bacon, 1984).

While the changes are underway, a reserve of "good will" is gradually consumed until results become visible. The longer the change takes to show results, the more "good will" is consumed. While "good will" exists, the organization can afford to be patient, but after it is exhausted, impatience takes over and the change effort typically falls apart. The problem is that organizations that need to change the most typically have the lowest reserves of good will. As a result, it is essential that results be demonstrated throughout the change effort to maintain the momentum of change.

• Real change only occurs when people's daily habits change; habits change only with time and practice. As a result, change based on "telling and teaching" almost never succeeds. Real change requires "doing."

Achieving improved results is not inconsistent with introducing change. In fact, achieving improved results while doing real work is essential to achieving sustainable results and is at the heart of the iterative approach. At every iteration assessment, lessons will be learned and acted upon to improve the project's performance and results. By its very nature, iterative and incremental development encourages learning by doing for everybody involved in the project, which enables the approach to support its own adoption and improvement.

The Role of Coaching

When a new way of working is introduced, it is important to support the transfer of knowledge and application of new ideas. Workshops are an effective way to do this because they enable people to learn in the context of doing real work, and they accelerate the rate at which people can be productive using the new techniques.

To feel confident in the change, people need to be able to focus on "doing" and not be distracted by "figuring out what to do." Experienced practitioners who lead people through the new behaviors, getting them to apply the new process by doing, must provide guidance and coaching. Having experienced coaches available to the project team provides confidence in the outcome by providing experienced resources for the project team—people who have already been successful on other projects. A sense of confidence in the outcome is essential to building resilience within the team so that team members can recover from the inevitable setbacks that occur in any change effort.

To facilitate experiential learning, coaches enable the team to focus on "execution" instead of process definition. In addition, there are several other benefits of this approach:

- It builds support for the change by creating real success early.
- It lets team members focus on "learning by doing" rather than sending them to classes and hoping they can put the knowledge into action on their own.
- It builds expertise within the team so that over time the team can support the new way of working without external help.
- It reduces the risk of failures, delays, and quality problems resulting from the team's learning by doing.
- It accelerates the learning process by eliminating much of the uncertainty, discussion, and trial-and-error associated with learning by doing.

Some coaching is usually necessary to enable project team success. This will vary from team to team, but typically these follow-on workshops are used to develop skills needed to execute the iteration plan. For example, in the Inception phase, project teams will need to understand how to understand the problem and create a vision for the solution; a workshop led by an experienced facilitator is often the most effective way to make progress toward this goal.

Sometimes the best coaches are on your own team in the form of the more experienced team members. Encouraging team members to work together to build team skills that improve team results also reinforces team cohesiveness. This does not happen accidentally, however; you will need to encourage it and plan for it.

Using the Iteration Plan to Provide a Roadmap for Change

The most effective method for introducing change is to tie the improvement effort directly to the work being performed. The most effective way to do this is to use the project and iteration planning effort (which must be done anyway) to drive the introduction of the new techniques just ahead of their need.

We have found that doing this through a series of focused workshops and subsequent hands-on mentoring jump-starts results and facilitates skills transfer. For planning evolutions and iterations, an initial full-day workshop to bootstrap the development plan and the initial iteration followed by half-day workshops at the start of each iteration to review results from the previous iteration and plan activities in the upcoming iteration has proven to be most effective. The structure and contents of these workshops are as follows:

- Early in the evolution, a workshop is needed to create the development plan and the initial iteration plan and to outline the approaches to be adopted to requirements and change management (often in the form of requirements management and change management plans). Iteration plans are defined so that just enough process is introduced to meet the objectives of the iteration and support the goals of the current "improvement cycle." In this way, the project team learns the new ways of working by applying them.

- At the transition between iterations, a workshop is needed to review iteration results, plan the next iteration, and identify issues and action plans. This can include making mid-project adjustments to the process used by the project, adjusting approaches as well as the pace of change. Sometimes the change will be too slow and the pacing can be accelerated; other times the project team will feel that the change was too fast and the improvement plans for future iterations will need to be scaled back.

The key to making improvements is to use the iteration plan itself to map the change activities *as well as* regular project activities. Change activities need to be viewed as integral to the project—tasks that the project does to achieve better results, not something external that detracts from results. If we don't believe that improved results will be derived from a change, why would we want to pursue it?

The iteration plan can be a powerful reinforcement to the change—or the means by which the change is undone: if the plan supports the change, it will tend to succeed, but if it fails to reinforce the new desired behaviors, the change will not happen no matter how much support is otherwise given.

As we have discussed, the project is structured into a series of iterations that establish a kind of heartbeat for the project, enabling it to set intermediate milestones to check progress, to establish points at which non-essential requirements can be scoped out, and to enable mid-course corrections to the project plan. This also acts as the heartbeat for change, enabling 1) short-term improvement objectives to be set, implemented, and assessed, 2) the change to be tested, and 3) mid-course corrections to made to the improvement plans.

Finally, planning is nothing if the execution of the plan is poor. Some people act as if a good plan will implement itself. In reality, a mediocre plan with excellent execution is better than an excellent plan with mediocre execution every time.

CONCLUSION

Adopting an iterative and incremental development approach is a fundamental change in working practices for the management team and everyone else involved in the project. Successful iterative and incremental development requires a progressive and adaptive approach to be taken to the management of the project and requires the whole team to embrace change and the continual improvement that this change will hopefully produce.

In any change effort, it is essential to demonstrate the value of the change as soon as possible to overcome resistance and build support for the change. The only way that can be done is by achieving the desired technical and business results quickly and efficiently. The fastest way to reach these results is to introduce the change as part of getting real work done; if the change is considered separate from the "real work," it will never produce results. With the guidance and leadership of an effective coach, and with the support of management to measure and reward positive results and positive change, teams can improve their process while getting real work done. Process improvement and getting results should not be considered mutually exclusive.

To expand beyond individual projects, you will need enlightened but benevolent dictatorship coupled with the demonstration through real results to all involved that the future can be better. It also requires leadership, real leadership—not the phony slogans of motivational posters, but roll-up-your-sleeves, hands-on leadership from the front action that shows that you have a stake in the outcome. No one is going to believe you if you sit on the sidelines cheering; you have to be in the game.

Iterative development is not hard, but changing the way that people work is. In this book, we have provided you with the background information and the practical guidance necessary to deliver better results through your software development efforts. The next step is yours: you now get to put these concepts into action. We hope that the approaches and techniques we have presented in this book will help you and your organization to succeed and thrive by achieving the full promise of iterative development.

● ● ●
SUGGESTED READING

Here, we suggest 10 books written for managers and decision makers that further illuminate the practical advantages of iterative, incremental software development. This is far from a comprehensive list. Our intent is to provide a selection of titles that extend our own discussion into various realms of software project management.

- Bittner, Kurt and Ian Spence. *Managing Iterative Software Development Projects*, Boston, MA: Addison-Wesley, 2007. Designed to reduce the anxiety and cost associated with software improvement, this book provides an easy and practical approach to organizing, estimating, staffing, and managing an iterative project. The authors offer a nonintrusive path toward improved results, without overwhelming you and your team.
- Brooks, Frederick P. *The Mythical Man-Month: Essays on Software Engineering, Second Edition*, Reading, MA: Addison-Wesley, 1995. A concise and insightful classic of software engineering management, this book should be required reading for every project manager up the management chain.

- Cantor, Murray. *Software Leadership: A Guide to Successful Software Development*, Boston, MA: Addison-Wesley, 2001. Full of insights into the essence of software, this book is about the art of successful leadership in the field of software development. Cantor explains principles of iterative technique, and helps new managers understand the flexible nature of planning, replanning, and executing in a competitive environment.

- DeMarco, Tom. *Controlling Software Projects: Management, Measurement & Estimation*, New York, NY: Yourdon Press, 1982.
  Beginning with the now-famous statement "You can't control what you can't measure," this book is a good analysis of how measurement can help managers understand, predict, and deliver software projects.

- DeMarco, Tom and Timothy Lister. *Peopleware: Productive Projects and Teams, Second Edition*, New York, NY: Dorset House Publishing Company, 1999.
  This book provides a good overview of a number of important "soft" factors in managing software development teams. Even though the first edition of this book is more than 20 years old, the situations and solutions DeMarco describes are still valid today.

- Gentle, Michael. *IT Success!: Towards a New Model for Information Technology*, Hoboken, NJ: Wiley, 2007.
  Addressing the problems encountered in software development from a management perspective, this book describes how projects—and IT in general—are funded and measured, and why a traditional approach is a large part of the problem that IT teams face. Gentle proposes a different relationship between customer and IT/software vendors that more resembles a partnership.

- Larman, Craig. *Agile and Iterative Development: A Manager's Guide*, Boston, MA: Addison-Wesley, 2003.

An exhaustive examination of the major methods in use for software development, this book demonstrates inadequacies of the waterfall software development lifecycle for managing object-oriented software projects, and advocates a variety of agile approaches instead.

- Marasco, Joe. *The Software Development Edge: Essays on Managing Successful Projects*, Boston, MA: Addison-Wesley, 2005.
  Collected and updated from their original appearance in *The Rational Edge* ezine, these essays capture decades of in-the-trenches experience across a broad spectrum of software topics. Marasco uses mathematics, physics, common sense, storytelling, and humor to provide a unique perspective on delivering software.
- Royce, Walker. *Software Project Management: A Unified Framework*, Reading, MA: Addison-Wesley, 1998.
  Further elaborating on the discussion in Part II of the current book, Royce provides a clear and provocative discussion of the economics, metrics, and management strategies needed to plan and execute software project successfully.
- Yourdon, Edward. *Death March, Second Edition*, Upper Saddle River, N.J.: Prentice Hall, 2003.
  A cautionary tale for what happens when you work the old way. Yourdon demonstrates the perils of sticking to a plan for the sake of the plan, especially when internal politics and fear are part of the equation.

INDEX

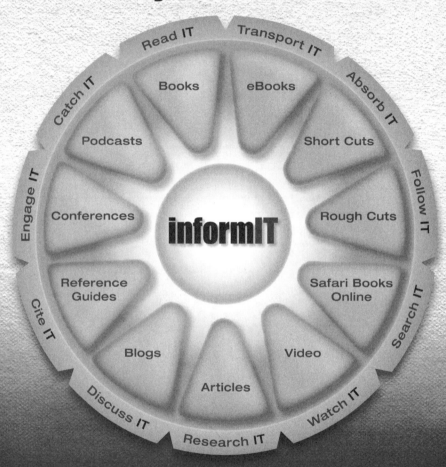

FREE Online Edition

Your purchase of *The Economics of Iterative Software Development: Steering Toward Better Business Results* includes access to a free online edition for 45 days through the Safari Books Online subscription service. Nearly every Addison-Wesley Professional book is available online through Safari Books Online, along with more than 5,000 other technical books and videos from publishers such as Cisco Press, Exam Cram, IBM Press, O'Reilly, Prentice Hall, Que, and Sams.

SAFARI BOOKS ONLINE allows you to search for a specific answer, cut and paste code, download chapters, and stay current with emerging technologies.

Activate your FREE Online Edition at www.informit.com/safarifree

> **STEP 1:** Enter the coupon code: HBRCIWH.

> **STEP 2:** New Safari users, complete the brief registration form. Safari subscribers, just log in.

If you have difficulty registering on Safari or accessing the online edition, please e-mail customer-service@safaribooksonline.com